Planting the
Peace Virus

Early Intervention to Prevent
Violence in Schools

Robyn Hromek

Lucky Duck is more than a publishing house and training agency. George Robinson and Barbara Maines founded the company in the 1980s when they worked together as a head and psychologist developing innovative strategies to support challenging students.

They have an international reputation for their work on bullying, self-esteem, emotional literacy and many other subjects of interest to the world of education.

George and Barbara have set up a regular news-spot on the website. Twice yearly these items will be printed as a newsletter. If you would like to go on the mailing list to receive this then please contact us:

e-mail newsletter@luckyduck.co.uk website www.luckyduck.co.uk

ISBN: 1 904 315 36 4

www.luckyduck.co.uk

Commissioning Editor: George Robinson
Editorial team: Mel Maines, Sarah Lynch, Wendy Ogden
Designer: Helen Weller
Cover: Barbara Maines

Printed in the UK by Antony Rowe Limited

Contents

Planting the Peace Virus

Early Intervention to Prevent Violence in Schools

The Peace Virus

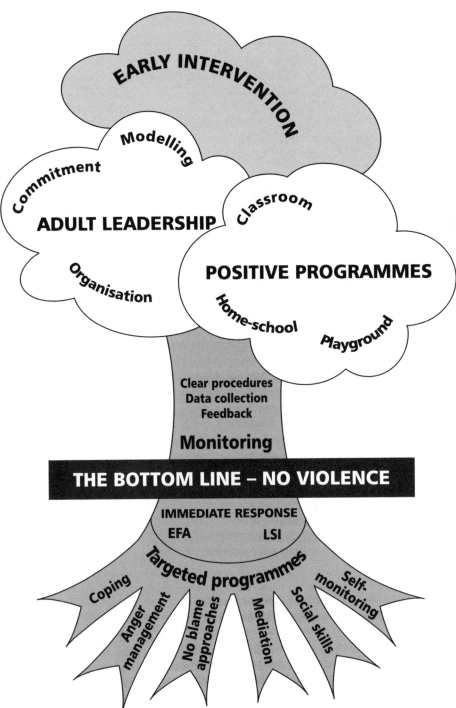

EARLY INTERVENTION

Modelling

Commitment

ADULT LEADERSHIP

Organisation

Classroom

POSITIVE PROGRAMMES

Home-school

Playground

**Clear procedures
Data collection
Feedback**

Monitoring

THE BOTTOM LINE – NO VIOLENCE

IMMEDIATE RESPONSE

EFA   LSI

Targeted programmes

Coping

Anger management

No blame approaches

Mediation

Social skills

Self-monitoring

If problems persist, see a doctor, therapist, CLINICAL INTERVENTION...

Introduction

This book tells the story of how a school planted a seed of peace that grew and rippled over the years. A reflective, narrative style tells what it was like for us, followed by critical research into early intervention, violence, emotional resilience, leadership and school change. Mind maps are included at the beginning of each section as a summary. The ideas presented are broadly based on those used by a primary school in New South Wales, Australia. Violence and harassment reduced over time and the school's efforts were recognised through a national antiviolence award (1998). The focus was on early intervention and the socio-emotional development of children aged 5 to 12. The terms 'violence' and 'aggression' are used interchangeably throughout and refer to hostile acts of a physical, verbal, or psycho-social nature, that is, hitting, biting, kicking, fighting, intimidation, social exclusion, threats, sexual harassment, etc. Bullying is viewed as an aggressive behaviour that is repeated, unjustified, oppressive and characterised by an imbalance of power favouring the perpetrator. It is important for school communities to develop an understanding of what they mean when they use these terms. The examples and scenarios are anecdotal and not based on any particular persons or events.

The story so far...

I was working as an educational psychologist at a large school – 600 children – in a coastal tourist town. It was a great school and a great town but the demographics were changing. Historically, the town evolved from whaling and forestry to being a hub for alternative lifestyles after the Nimbin Aquarius festival in the seventies. By the nineties, the 'hippies' were still in town but the property prices were rising. Our school population was highly mobile – up to one third came and went each year. When we started keeping records, there were about seven or eight violent incidents recorded each week and teasing levels were high, with sometimes 20 or more children involved in harassing one child.

Our response to violence and harassment evolved over time and came into focus when 'detention and punishment' cycles proved ineffective in reducing playground violence. When I arrived, the school had an active team of teachers called the 'welfare committee' who were using a case management approach to children with difficulties. Most of my work was negotiated with this team and the senior staff. We began talking about the problems in the playground and decided to start a dialogue about violence and how to address it in general staff meetings. As discussion proceeded, our response to violence took form and became a school priority. Shared understandings about violence developed and our response plan changed and grew as our understandings changed. We talked about the difference between detention and attention, punishment, shame and revenge cycles and the role of assistance and remediation. The whole staff supported a bottom line of 'No Violence' and we worked out an immediate response to provide consistency of teacher response. Inappropriate playtime behaviour was described and placed in a hierarchy with a range of responses assigned for each level. Basically, we all knew what to do if or when violence occurred.

Our senior staff used a range of approaches when working with children in crisis – mediation, conflict resolution, strengths-based, solution-focused, no-blame interviews, emotional coaching, mentoring, restitution and referrals to targeted programmes. I was closely involved with developing and organising remedial programmes – targeted, brief interventions that were often run at lunch-time. Activities included therapeutic games, mediation, role-playing, modelling, problem-solving and blame-free interviews – all with an attitude of fun, respect and curiosity.

The playground team met weekly to evaluate data, refine our responses and get organised. Despite being very busy, I think we must have enjoyed it – the coffee, the catch-up, the minutes of the last meeting, the reports to the whole staff, etc., etc., etc… We created protocols, letters to send home, quick-tick checklists and our wonderful playground bag – a shoulder bag we used to hold the bits and pieces of the playground programme. Gradually our preventative programmes took shape. Teachers began using social skills lessons and discussed playtime behaviour with the children in class and at assemblies. We worked out an induction process for new teachers, parents and children. We designed positive playground programmes and applied incentives liberally. Children's leadership skills were developed through programmes like peer mediation, student representative council, buddy-mentoring and peer tutoring.

Most children responded positively to the universal, proactive strategies we put in place. Assistance was provided for children with difficulties through targeted programmes. Violence reduced to about three incidents per week by term four – after a few years, this level dropped to about one per week, if that. Parental involvement was encouraged and actively supported early in the process, especially if children were experiencing behaviour difficulties. If a child continued to experience difficulties after the preventative and targeted programmes, then specialist medical, psychological or social support was sought. An interagency case management approach was used to obtain the best understanding of the child and to help design individual management plans. This tertiary level of response helped identify children with organic syndromes, mental health problems or other mitigating factors like child abuse or disadvantage due to poverty or racism.

At first, we all – playground team, senior staff, peer mediators, teachers, parents, carers – were extremely busy, collecting and analysing data, running programmes, supporting initiatives and mediating. But over a year or so, the workload reduced as more and more children adopted peaceful ways to manage emotion and work through 'social and emotional challenges'. Eventually, the playground team didn't need to meet so often – once a fortnight to monitor the programme, process the data and monitor children with individual management plans. Gradually, there was less and less work for peer mediators so we began to think of new leadership avenues for them. Data collection and evaluation became part of our culture and we could see how violence and harassment were declining and shifting over time.

Looking back on what I have just written, we seem like an impressive lot – but we were just a bunch of teachers trying different ideas to reduce violence and harassment in our school. We were patient (some would say 'long suffering') and realistic about how far and how fast we could go. We had our champions who led the way on different strategic ideas – but also we had our many who maintained the bag, or sharpened the pencils, or entered the data…we all just did the 'bit' we could. We made up a bigger picture puzzle out of which the Peace Virus grew.

About the Peace Virus

The Peace Virus helps schools uphold standards against violence in all its forms and uses democratic, respectful ways of working together. Through universal, targeted and clinical programmes, a social milieu is created where the norm is to use prosocial strategies to solve interpersonal difficulties. Theoretical underpinnings to this approach lie in the social cognitive theories of Alfred Bandura (1986), the mediated learning approaches of Vygotsky(1986) and Feuerstein (1980) and the life-space interview approaches of Fritz Redl (1966) and Nicholas Long (in Wood & Long, 1991). The model put forward in this book is an early intervention model that encourages adults to model respect, act as emotional coaches for children lacking in socio-emotional skills, and guide them through the problem-solving process. Universal, preventative programmes are broadcast across classrooms and playgrounds and when difficulties emerge targeted, remedial programmes are provided. Parents, carers and community agencies are engaged when problems persist. This systematic approach serves as a diagnostic tool as children with persistent behaviour difficulties are identified and referred for early intervention. The following facets that make up the Peace Virus are explored in this book:

Adult leadership: Leadership is crucial to foster a high standard of interpersonal relations and to implement improvement programmes. A respectful and dignified attitude sets the tone for the school. Enthusiasm for ideas, provision of resources and support for staff is needed as they address the needs of the school. Open discussion sets the priorities of the school and keeps the community involved and informed. Ideally, leadership comes from the headteacher, but any inspired person or group can lead the way by raising issues in staff and parent meetings and by adopting non-violent, respectful attitudes.

Commitment: When violence is an issue in a school, communities must prioritise immediate and careful attention to the situation and develop a response plan. Other programmes may have to wait until the school is deemed safe. Every adult has a part to play in what may seem to be a long, endless path. Without commitment, projects fail, people become discouraged and violence remains an accepted means of solving problems.

Early intervention: Sociologists and medical experts conclude that the answer to many of society's intractable problems is early intervention into poverty and cycles of disadvantage (Perry, 1991). Not only does early intervention benefit a child's life-outcomes, it builds social capital and is cost effective. Interagency collaboration between health, housing, education and social support agencies is necessary to provide effective services to families early. While early intervention is cost effective, the number of children needing help in some communities is enormous, leading to worker overload. Political decisions, government policy, community action and financial support are required to make a real difference to poverty and disadvantage. While much is outside the school's control, they can still have an effect by inviting other agencies to planning meetings where a holistic approach is taken to meet physical, social, psychological and emotional needs.

Modelling: Adults constantly model behaviour to children and, at times, inadvertently model authoritarian and 'power based' stances. The words we use and the actions we take provide an ongoing sample of behaviour for children to copy or reject. Language is a fundamental behaviour and as such forms our understandings of the world. Words can be used to scaffold a child's socio-emotional development. The practice of mindfulness and reflection helps us change old patterns. 'Scripts' can also be used to develop co-operative, respectful language patterns until they become natural to our way of relating and to help children develop adaptive thought processes.

Teamwork: Working in teams shares the workload and sustains the energy required to change school cultures. Time, resources, professional development and support structures are required to support the work teams undertake on behalf of the school community. Teamwork provides leadership opportunities and when democratic practices are instituted, team members have a chance to design and try innovative ideas.

Parental involvement: Collaboration between the home, school and community is essential to meet the learning needs of children. Having a flexible range of procedures to involve parents and carers fosters an attitude of shared responsibility. Open communication and perspective taking by both the home and school creates a climate that encourages solution-focused and strengths-based approaches to problems.

Effective interventions: Intervention is costly in effort, time and money, so proven school-wide interventions targeted to local situations are required. The most cost effective interventions are universal, preventative programmes, like teaching socio-emotional skills in the classroom, positive playground programmes, parent resource centres. Secondary level or targeted, remedial programmes are used with children who need extra direct tuition and closer monitoring, for example, small group work, behaviour contracts, mediation, anger management and values. If violence continues after this focused attention, then tertiary level or clinical interventions are required. Parents or carers, health professionals, educationalists, community and social workers have a role in determining the nature of the difficulties and developing individual response plans with ongoing monitoring for these children.

Response plans: A response plan sets out clearly the proactive and reactive programmes and immediate teacher responses used when violence is an issue. Having a response plan ensures consistency of teacher response and fairness to children. Plans evolve as playground data is analysed and the needs of the school shift. When violence occurs, consistent and immediate steps are followed that are known to teachers, students, parents or carers, for example, children are immediately withdrawn from the playground, interviewed by a teacher and referred to targeted programmes. The professional development of teachers and the involvement of parents and carers are crucial parts of the plan.

Monitoring: Systematic monitoring and evaluation of programmes through data collection and analysis is pivotal in focusing an ongoing response to violence. Simple and practical strategies are needed to make it easier for staff to carry out this vital step. Close monitoring of the playground allows clear procedures to be developed and is the basis of feedback to the wider community. Monitoring also acts as a deterrent, in that children who know they are being observed adjust and monitor their own behaviour.

In conclusion, there are many ways to reach the goal of peaceful co-operation in schools. By adapting some of the ideas presented and maintaining proven, successful programmes already in use, it is possible to meet the specific needs of individual schools. Some of the terms used should be altered to reflect local culture (peer leaders, welfare team, welfare teachers, crisis intervention teachers, attention room, etc.). While the ideas presented are largely cost neutral, a lot depends on the good will and commitment of a core group of teachers. The work would be easier if human and financial resources were available to schools as part of a broader social policy of early intervention into violence. It would have been less taxing if local education authorities had made available resources like trained personnel to advise and train staff in the delivery of effective programmes and if local services clubs had invested in our projects. Easy access to community-based programmes would also have improved things for families in crisis.

Some cautionary words: Having begun the task of changing the culture of violence in a school, do not stop, especially if children have been encouraged to confront violence through help seeking or assertiveness training. Children who ask for help must be assisted until the problem is resolved, otherwise dangerous situations may arise. For example, aggressors may make threats to 'get them' after school or 'bash them' if they tell. Also, be aware of ways in which violence can go 'underground' or be socialised into less obvious forms, for example, physical violence may be extinguished from a child's behaviour repertoire only to be replaced by verbal or emotional abuse.

Some words of encouragement: The first few months and possibly years of implementing a violence response plan can be intense and busy times, depending on pre-existing levels of violence. It helps to see this intense phase of close monitoring and immediate response as a temporary means to an end, a transitory phase to a more settled era. Also, do not expect to be able to do everything at once and be encouraged that every step taken works to reduce violence and harassment, especially in the first few years of a child's schooling. School communities need to believe that violence is neither inevitable nor acceptable and, through appropriate culture and instruction, can be substantially eliminated from the school.

Section 1

The Gardeners – Adult Leadership

Adult Leadership

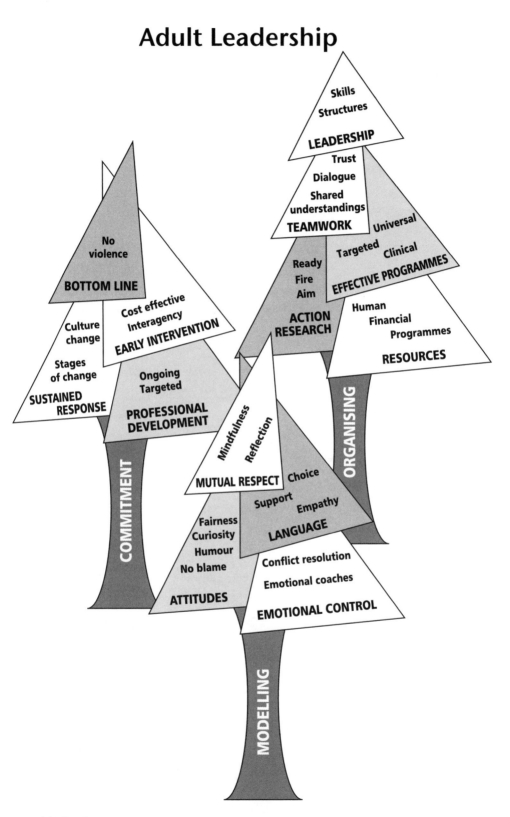

Skills
Structures
LEADERSHIP

Trust
Dialogue
Shared understandings
TEAMWORK

Universal
Targeted   Clinical
EFFECTIVE PROGRAMMES

No violence
BOTTOM LINE

Ready
Fire
Aim
ACTION RESEARCH

Human
Financial
Programmes
RESOURCES

Culture change
Cost effective
Interagency
EARLY INTERVENTION

Stages of change
SUSTAINED RESPONSE

Ongoing
Targeted
PROFESSIONAL DEVELOPMENT

COMMITMENT

ORGANISING

Mindfulness
Reflection
MUTUAL RESPECT   Choice

Support
Empathy
LANGUAGE

Fairness
Curiosity
Humour
No blame
ATTITUDES

Conflict resolution
Emotional coaches
EMOTIONAL CONTROL

MODELLING

Commitment To Non-violence

The story continues...

Our school was quite large with about 600 children and 25 teachers plus support staff. I was there in my role as educational psychologist for one and a half days per week. The welfare team (playground team) was made up of eight to ten volunteer teachers who met weekly to discuss the welfare of the students with a focus on playground issues. We began raising the management of violence as an issue in our team meetings and took the discussion to the whole-staff meetings. The senior staff were committed to addressing violence – they attended playground meetings, learnt to use mediation, supported preventative and targeted, remedial programmes and provided administrative support for keeping records. Debates were open and at times, strong and animated, but all opinions were respected and discussed. Agreements were made and remade about how to respond to violence. Our violence response plan was designed and modified by the playground team, in consultation with the whole staff and parents and carers through forums like the 'Parents and Citizens' committee. Newsletters and the School Handbook set out the school's response to violence and harassment.

Working with the school community was an ongoing process. There was an atmosphere of respect and support for parents and carers, including especially those with difficult children, which made it easier for them to talk to the senior teachers. Hearing the voice of parents and carers as a 'body' proved a little more elusive, with the main forum being the Parents and Citizens Committee. Over the years, parents and carers were surveyed on various issues – with varying response rates. A particularly successful strategy was the 'quality review' process available to schools from the department of education. Schools could request an independent review of their school programmes by a team of experienced teachers and headteachers. As part of this 'quality review', interviews were conducted with parents, carers, teachers and students that were analysed to give the headteacher a great basis on which to build a school improvement plan. The anonymity of the process and independence of the survey analysis meant we had an honest reflection of people's perceptions of the school.

I was able to negotiate my role in the school to support the violence prevention and remediation programmes. This meant that some of my more 'traditional' roles as educational psychologist were set aside for a while, for example, IQ tests, measurement of academic skills, consultation on individual learning plans. The school agreed to exhaust other resources before referring less urgent cases to me, leaving more time to follow-up violent incidents as a priority. Over time, I was able to present research-based alternatives to staff who were, to greater and lesser extents, open to understanding and using preventative and remedial approaches. Gradually, as the statistics showed less violence, enthusiasm and support grew…

Outmoded Paradigms

Historically, pedagogy has relied on discipline and punishment. Competitive systems of learning and individual effort have been paramount when defining academic success. Most of us have experienced these practices to some extent and can, when faced with challenges, fall back on these approaches. Many schools operate on the questionable belief that 'getting tough' on violence or disruptive behaviour communicates to children that this behaviour will not be tolerated and punishment will teach them to behave in prosocial ways. Unfortunately, over-reliance on punishment and exclusion seems to create a negative, adversarial school environment and breed a cycle of resentment and revenge. Research shows that punishment based interventions usually lead to an increase in problem behaviours (Donnellan et al, 1988, Mayer et al, 1990). Educators and parents or carers most likely agree with a philosophy of non-violence in our schools and homes. We might also agree that positive, organised, respectful, safe schools enhance teaching and learning. However, examination of some of our interactions and practices produces evidence of violence in words and actions. We need a change of culture. Peaceful communities begin with us: headteachers, teachers, parents, carers, helpers and visitors, all need to show children we can live together with mutual respect. We create our social environments with every shared interaction. Being committed to non-violence requires honest reflection on how we respond to each other. This is hard when we are dealing with violent and disrespectful children or problematic adults. Nevertheless, with each interaction we model response styles to children; whether diplomatic and respectful, or authoritarian and aggressive. The Peace Virus starts with respect shown through the words we use, our facial expressions, body language and actions used in our lives together in the school community. These outward signs are windows into the values, beliefs and attitudes that shape our schools.

Groundswell of Change

This is good news and not so good news. The good news is that it is the adults of the community who need to begin the work of reflection upon our interactions. The bad news is that it is easy to forget we are modelling to children, especially when tired, frustrated or when others have forgotten their manners too. Each school community will have different levels of commitment to non-violence and you may find yourself as part of a minority who believe schools, along with families and communities, have a central role to play in preventing antisocial behaviour. It is easy to feel over whelmed by the sheer volume of violence around us: world events, television, movies, computer games, print media, our homes, schools and workplaces. It may seem too big a challenge to tackle, especially when we see well-meaning people engage in practices that support the disempowerment of others. It seems even harder when violence is used by the nations of the world to resolve their conflicts. Whatever the case, if we are personally committed to non-violence, we can start in the roles we occupy with small, targeted strategies. In our part of the network that creates a school community or family, we can use respectful words, model emotional control, protect children from emotional harm, use problem-solving approaches and join with like-minded people to put in place structures and programmes supportive of a peaceful environment. We can join the playground team; or do extra playground duty to release someone else to run the 'attention room'; or teach socio-emotional skills; or adopt democratic approaches in the classroom. As witnessed in recent world events, a groundswell of people around the world is demanding their nations use peaceful ways to resolve conflict. Be encouraged to make a stand against violence in our communities and prepared to put in some tough work for a time to support the growth of peace. Olweus (1993), a seminary researcher in the area of violence and harassment in schools came to the encouraging conclusion that most efforts towards elimination of violence will have a positive impact. As simple a step as talking about bullying at assembly, or showing anti-bullying videos reduces teasing and harassment. How much more effective will a co-ordinated effort be using proven methods? Commitment grows in school communities where there is:

- supportive and visionary leadership
- frequent and democratic discussion among stake holders, including children, leading to shared understandings about concepts, words and response
- data driven management that focuses on intervention and triggers celebration
- a school-wide response plan with proactive and targeted programmes set out clearly
- support for antiviolence programmes – time and resources for teamwork
- structures and resources to support the ongoing cycle of implementation and evaluation
- school improvement through professional development of teachers and parents or carers
- an understanding of the long-term nature of improvement plans
- celebration of success along the way.

Stages of Change

We need to replace punitive responses to aggressive students with comprehensive, remedial and sustained interventions that are culturally sensitive, school wide, supported through teamwork and delivered as early as possible in children's lives. In the reality that is our schools, we all know this is a big task. The process involves patience, talking, planning, finding resources and implementing effective, integrated approaches. Often schools abandon effective intervention programmes because the time and effort involved in their implementation is perceived as too costly (Witt et al, 1983; Witt et al, 1985). There are several stages in the transition from violent to peaceful schools and it helps to remember that the hardest phase of changing cultures is transitory. The first stage involves collecting data and identifying problems in the school through wide consultation and observation. Schools require accurate information on types and frequency of violence, individuals involved, which classes are most represented, and the 'hotspots' where it is occurring. This important step informs the school's 'violence response plan'. The second stage involves working collaboratively to plan proactive and reactive responses: consulting other schools, involving specialist teachers, educational psychologists, local education authorities and locating effective resources. The third stage involves ongoing policing and monitoring of violence while nurturing a new culture through proactive and reactive programmes. This is the most intense stage and may last for some time, depending on pre-existing levels of violence. Once violence has reduced, the final stage of maintaining the response plan is reached. The school's priorities shift towards projects that may have been put on hold. Eventually, as children progress through school they become role models for younger children, bringing with them socio-emotional skills they have learned along the way. An environment exists where children manage social difficulties in prosocial ways, or at least know how to get assistance when needed. New children enter a community that is immersed in non-violent approaches and are supported in their adjustment to the status quo through monitoring of their integration. Children with extra support needs generally find the environment less fractious, making their inclusion in the school community more successful.

Trusting that our efforts will change the school's culture helps to make the work meaningful and a little easier. It also gives us confidence that allocating valuable resources to the task of reducing violence in our schools is not in vain.

Early Intervention

Early intervention is the key to good outcomes for children from disadvantaged families. Much evidence supports the effectiveness of early intervention programmes in terms of both life outcomes for children and economic considerations (Behrman, 1995; Karoly et al, 1998; Perry, 1996). Long-term outcomes of early intervention include prevention of delinquency, reduction in teen pregnancies and violent crime and increased school success (Behrman, 1995; Greenwood, 1995; Zigler et al., 1992). Governments are beginning to lend support to structures that bring together community agencies like education, social services, health and housing in an intervention model to support families with young children, for example, Families First, NSW, Australia; Sure Start, United Kingdom; Ireland National Children's Plan, HeadStart, USA. Walker et al (1996) see early intervention into the lives of 'at risk' children as essential in stemming the tide of youth violence. They re-conceptualise the role of schools in preventing antisocial behaviour among children and youth, seeing schools as:

- co-ordinators of collaboration between schools, families, social service agencies, medical clinics
- providers of generic or universal approaches to reducing risk factors for antisocial behaviour and enhancing protective factors
- targeting of 'at risk' children early in their lives with remedial programmes instead of exclusionary practices.

Unfortunately, most 'at-risk' students with behavioural problems are referred to, and access services well after the point when their problems can be successfully remediated (Kazdin, 1987). That is why it is important for primary schools to screen and identify 'at-risk' children early in their school careers and provide comprehensive, targeted interventions that can make a difference. In addition, schools with nurturing cultures provide havens for children with troubled home lives, adding to their emotional resilience. Often schools are the most predictable, consistent, normalised and prosocial environments available to children on a daily basis. Schools can only play this role effectively in partnership with families and community agencies and with support from the wider community and government. Education authorities and governments have a responsibility to develop a continuum of alternative programmes and placements in order to keep children engaged with schooling for as long as possible. Early intervention works; it must be made a high priority for ongoing funding, policy and service delivery by all agencies.

Open Discussion and Teamwork

At the basis of successful school improvement is a strong culture of teamwork and ongoing professional development. A sense of collegiality and mutual support creates a culture of trust and confidence among staff and new ideas are more readily accepted. Enthusiasm remains high when recognition is given for effort and where success is celebrated. A good sense of humour and fun goes a long way to uplift each other during times of great effort. Open discussion develops the shared understandings necessary for consistency of response to violence and data collection.

Honest discussion will lead the way towards agreement and co-operation. There is every chance that some will think punishment is entirely appropriate or that boys should be left to 'thrash it out, man to man'. Differing beliefs and values exist and some may be held passionately. Respectful responses that present alternative frameworks are needed. It may be helpful to invite experts like psychologists, doctors, therapists or social workers to help present alternative ways of managing violence and harassment. Complete agreement is not possible or required to initiate the types of changes that will support the growth of a new culture. People gradually adopt new attitudes in the face of successful practices. Discussion of the following topics develops shared understandings of the terms being used and the nature of violence in the school:

- What are the main problems at our school? Where do they happen? When? This discussion helps create the setting for other discussions.
- What do we mean by the terms 'teasing', 'harassmen', 'bullying'?

- What is violence? What are the different types of violence? Violence can emerge in many forms including physical, verbal, social and emotional.

- How are violence and 'rough play' different? How is temper different to violence? Should they be managed and recorded differently? Discussion of these issues helps create shared understandings and operationalise the terms being used by teachers.

- In what ways is violence different for boys and girls? Boys tend to use physical violence more often to solve their problems than do girls, while girls tend to use social isolation and words more readily than boys do. This discussion underpins the importance of responding to all aspects of violence.

- Will teaching conflict resolution lead to the feminisation of boys? Should boys be allowed to 'fight it out'? Are the 'talking therapies' like mediation going to make boys more like girls? How can we support 'boys' education' initiatives while reducing physical violence?

- How can we be supportive of special needs children in our school, especially those with emotional difficulties? What is the nature of emotional disability, autism, conduct disorders, etc? What do we need to do differently?

- What is the difference between discipline and punishment and how do they affect behaviour? How can our words be punishing? How are cycles of shame and revenge kept going?

- How should children make restitution for anti-social actions? Why is restitution important to psychological health?

- What is the difference between assertiveness and aggression? Is our body language reflecting how we want to communicate?

- What role should adults take in helping children solve problems? How can we mediate their learning without robbing them of the learning experience?

- What is the role for children as leaders and mediators? Is our school ready for peer leadership programmes like mediation?

Teachers as Learners

Teachers are facing the most exciting time for their profession in the modern era. Again, the teacher's role is changing. As technology increasingly takes over some of their more traditional roles, like 'subject master' and administrator, teachers will be left with the tasks of teaching students about critical thinking and providing empathic support. Critical thinking is arguably the most significant feature of development for future citizens and employees, while having a teacher who knows and understands their students and who is passionate about their learning will support the development of the whole person. As the information age gains momentum, teachers must remain learners, adopting 'action research' approaches whereby they change and grow in what they do in their classroom. They must become active researchers into the 'what' and 'how' of their pedagogy. Ongoing professional development will become even more crucial for teachers to remain a driving force for innovation and research into teaching practice.

While information is increasing and changing, and teaching practice changes to meet this challenge, one role will remain the same: that of mentor. Teachers generally have an empathetic, personal understanding of their students, enabling them to guide them in subject choice, study skills, motivation and social and emotional development. While this is a traditional role for teachers, new ways of dealing with interpersonal difficulties are necessary. As the demands and roles of teaching changes, teachers will increasingly need skills in areas like:

- conflict resolution
- mediation
- emotional coaching
- no-blame approaches to interviewing
- child psychology – motivation, learning, developmental stages
- emotional literacy – emotional vocabulary, identifying and labelling emotion
- interagency collaboration
- quality pedagogy.

Modelling Respect

The story continues...

The calm, confident and respectful attitudes of many at our school were examples to us all, including the children. We hadn't really formally talked about the process of modelling but there was a cordial and respectful atmosphere among the staff, parents and carers on the whole. Staff differences were dealt with in confidential and respectful ways, sometimes involving conflict resolution and mediation by the senior staff.

While reading about peer mediation I came across social cognitive and mediated learning ideas. I could see how important language was when working with children and began to observe how well they responded to respectful management. Listening to children with a non-judgmental attitude, seeing their point of view, acknowledging their strengths and values, encourages them to take responsibility for their actions. I really enjoyed working with the peer mediators. Children love being given responsibility and learning about new, respectful ways of interacting. With the peer mediators, we had a whole lot more models of respectful problem-solvers in the playground. Usually a staff member mediated the more complicated or intractable cases.

Modelling respectful attitudes and processes to children was a crucial step in changing the culture. It helped us maintain professional relationships with each other and this 'rubbed off' on the kids. I came across the 'educator's Hippocratic oath' recently: discipline without humiliation; criticise without destroying self-worth; praise without judging; and express anger without hurting (source unknown).

We are always modelling; children watch and listen to everything we do and say. They will reflect the interaction they observe and are more likely to use non-violent ways of resolving conflict when their social environment models language and practices conducive to emotional control and problem-solving. As we work with children in respectful ways, as we model emotional control and use words carefully, as we mediate and problem-solve, we demonstrate a range of skills for working and living together.

Theoretical Underpinnings

According to the social cognitive theories of Bandura (1986), children's learning depends on their social milieu as much as their internal, inherited characteristics. By observing and imitating the interactions of those around them, children integrate behaviour into a framework of internal meaning. He concluded that programmes based on modelling, coaching, behavioural rehearsal and social reinforcement yield significant results. Vygotsky (1976), a child development theorist, postulated the importance of language as a mediating factor between a child and an event. He suggested adults help children develop higher level thinking skills through a process called 'mediated learning', that is, the process of guiding a child through learning experiences by using language to help create the thought concepts needed to meet challenges. Mediated learning experiences provide the resources a child might use to solve problems without explicitly telling them how to solve the problems. If one simply gives the solution to a child, an opportunity to develop higher level thinking skills is lost. By allowing the child to make associations between previous experiences and the resources around them, they learn important developmental skills. Words and language are 'resources' that can be used to surround events in a child's experience. They are symbols that assist in the formulation of thought constructs that influence future responses.

Mediated Learning Experiences (MLE) are planned so that the right kind of interaction occurs between the teacher and student to develop effective thinking skills that lead to autonomous and independent learners (Skuy, 1997). The model extends to socio-emotional development as well as linguistic, numeric and physical development. As adults in a child's world, we model language (emotional vocabulary) and communication skills (listening, clarifying, creating and evaluating options) that scaffold their socio-emotional growth. Programmes based on modelling, coaching, behaviour rehearsal, role-plays, and social reinforcement yield significant results in teaching social skills and non-violence to children. Thus is the responsibility of child-raising shared by the broader social network in which children live and learn.

Mutual Respect

When asked about their favourite teachers, children frequently mention the quality of respect. In turn, teachers and parents or carers often bemoan the lack of respect children hold for adults. Respect is manifest in the way people acknowledge each other's rights and responsibilities. It is reflected in the words, attitudes and actions used when interacting. By speaking to children with respect, we model behaviour that improves interpersonal relationships, increasing the chance that they will choose similar, respectful behaviour to resolve interpersonal conflict. In order to receive respect, we must give respect. Creating respect for adult leadership involves:

- having clear behavioural expectations, displayed and discussed at a 'calm' time
- applying natural and logical consequences that are moderate and consistent
- using optimistic and supportive language
- looking for strengths and values
- allowing a 'cool off' period before addressing issues – emotional first-aid
- assisting with problem-solving
- adopting a matter of fact, curious attitude
- not engaging in arguments with children
- ensuring opportunities for restitution are available.

Mindfulness and Reflection

Mindfulness and reflection are self-awareness strategies that are valuable components of professional behaviour and help us develop an awareness of the school, work and home environments we are co-creating. Being self-aware means that, in some way, we are observers of our thoughts, words and feelings and tune into our body's sensations. This self-monitoring is the first step towards emotional control, a skill much needed when working with children. The most difficult part is remembering to practise mindfulness. A helpful tactic is to catch oneself mid-sentence, take note of the words, their intent, and their effect on others and later, at a quiet time, reflect on the interaction. Examine different ways of saying things and look for the emotive content. Reflective practice involves the process of observation, reflection, analysis, critical debate, investigation and experimentation. Smyth (1997) sees engaging in critique of one's teaching practice as a way of opening up the transformative possibilities implicit in the social context of classrooms and schooling. Smyth states:

> 'Teachers are not working with inert materials that respond according to some pre-determined rules. Students are continually engaging in dialectical processes with their teachers and through this process coming to create as well as share in the culture common to both of them.' (Smyth, 1987, p 16)

Teachers are increasingly using this phenomenological approach to examining their classroom practice (Holly, 1989; Schon, 1983; Smyth, 1986, 1992). Some schools have formalised reflective practice by making the last ten minutes of the school day a time for teachers and students to reflect on the day's achievements and to set goals for the next day.

Language

We need to be mindful of the words and body language we model. Carefully chosen language is vital to producing the kinds of understandings that help children make prosocial choices. Our language needs to reflect mutual respect, rights, responsibilities and choices. Through words, we create supportive environments that assume children can resolve conflict without violence and make restitution for their mistakes. Consider the following examples of language patterns and the underlying principles they reflect:

PROSOCIAL LANGUAGE	ANTISOCIAL LANGUAGE
Choice and responsibility "How did you come to the decision to hit him?" This question implies there was an element of choice and responsibility and invites communication.	**Accusatory** "Why did you hit him?" This question may have an accusatory element that makes children resentful and possibly limit communication.
Supportive approach "You will need to go to the 'chill out' room and work out a way to solve this problem." This implies the child is able to solve their problem and receive support if needed.	**Punitive approaches** "I'm putting you in detention." This implies punishment and if over used may lead to revenge cycles in children.
Empathy "How do you think she felt when you said that to her?" This statement invites the child to develop empathy for the other child and opens communication.	**Emotional violence** "Look what you have done, you've made her cry." The accusatory nature of this statement may make the child feel guilty or defensive leading to resentment and closed communication.
Problem-solving and restitution "What are some of the things you could do to try to meet this challenge?" This statement implies confidence in the child's ability to solve the problem and make restitution for their acts.	**Sarcasm** "You had better think of something good to explain this." There is an element of sarcasm in this statement with the implication that the child is not be able to solve the problem.

At first, structuring language seems strange and stilted but eventually becomes a more natural process, especially as more members of the community begin to reflect on the words they use. We need to avoid accusatory, sarcastic language. Violence appears in many ways and the tongue can be a subtle knife, cutting deep into the memory of a child. Remember cringing on hearing adults make thoughtless comments such as, 'Get out of my classroom!' or, 'I don't have to put up with you any longer', or, 'You're just not trying'. With a little thought and practice, it is possible to create an atmosphere of support and optimism through carefully chosen words thus enhancing children's emotional vocabulary.

We can help children develop the language of peace through modelling prosocial language, by reframing what they say to us in words that reflect responsibility and choice and by providing them with 'scripts'. Scripts are a useful tool to help us while we are still learning to use words that reflect choice, control and confidence. Scripts of positive self-talk help children learn language patterns that will assist self-monitoring. Vygotsky (1962) observed that children's self-talk or inner speech seemed to have a self-monitoring function. Scripts are samples of self-talk that children can use when dealing with problems such as anger, frustration or conflict. Scripts allow children to learn and use new word patterns that form the basis of new thought constructs. Teaching scripts to children provides them with ideas and positive self-talk to use in future problem-solving situations. For example, 'I'm getting help from the teacher if you keep annoying me' is less confronting and aggressive than saying, 'I'm telling on you'. Everyone is allowed to get help when needed. If a child says this confidently and walks away, they have demonstrated control and probably defused a tricky situation. Scripts work well in semi-structured situations like crisis interventions or therapeutic games.

Emotional Control

Words are crucial to the development of the thought constructs required to solve problems, and combined with body language, can model emotional control to children. Consider what is modelled through the words and actions in the following scenarios:

Teacher A sees two boys fighting in the playground. The following interaction takes place:

T. A   (Shouting) **Come here at once you two!! What do you think you are doing!!**

Boy 1   (Red faced and puffing) **He started it**

Boy 2   (Red faced and crying, tries to land another blow on Boy 1)

T. A   (shouting at the boys) **That's it! Go to the headteacher's office immediately!**

Superficially, the teacher has dealt with the violence. While probably agreeing with non-violence and the importance of intervention, the teacher's actions, words and tone reveal a degree of verbal violence, suggesting something of their beliefs and values. They might believe that violent children should be dealt with sternly and are reliant on adults to solve their problems or that there is no hope for them and they have no place in mainstream schools. The children may well have learnt some unintended lessons as well:

- Shouting at others is OK, especially if you are in the right.
- Tough language is OK, especially if you are in the right.
- Gathering information and listening is not very important.
- Children need adults to manage them.
- Verbal violence is a valid way to solve problems.

Consider this alternative dialogue for dealing with the same situation:

Teacher B sees two boys fighting in the playground. The following interaction occurs:

T. B   (Moving towards the boys) **Hold on boys – calm down now – take it easy – what's happening here?**

Boy 1   (Red faced and puffing) **He started it.**

Boy 2	(Red faced and crying, tries to land another blow on Boy 1)
T. B	**Hold on, hold on – take a deep breath, you're both upset – let's go get a drink of water and talk about what's happening here.**

In this scenario, the teacher has applied emotional first-aid and used language that reflects emotional control and problem-solving. The situation has been defused and the expectation is that both will have a chance to explain what the difficulty was and what helped them decide to solve the problem with violence. From these words and actions, we infer that this teacher believes children can learn to manage emotion and that modelling helps develop these skills. They might also believe adults can be emotional coaches and help them resolve interpersonal problems. They are likely to support inclusive educational practice and value the role they play in helping children become responsible citizens. They value non-violence and see the importance of intervening early into violent situations. From this encounter, the children may have learnt:

- It is possible to manage emotions.
- Adults want to help.
- Adults believe children can solve problems.
- Talking is an alternative to violence.
- Drinking water and walking might help manage anger.

Attitudes: Approaches that avoid issues of blame help maintain neutrality and fairness when working with children. These attitudes show a willingness to consider the perspectives of all stakeholders, ensuring equality among the children. Using humour and curiosity often defuses tension and reassures children of our positive regard for them. When adults view problems as opportunities for growth and acknowledge the values held by children they are released from the stifling effects of guilt, and more open to considering acts of restitution. With the right attitude, we help produce stress free environments in which children engage with us in the problem-solving process.

3

Getting Organised

The story continues...

It seemed like we were always organising – it was an ongoing process. We enjoyed our Tuesday mornings – they were sometimes lively but there was enough trust to express differing opinions and ideas. Most staff were not directly involved in creating the response plan, but when we came up with new ideas they were presented as drafts to the whole staff. Everyone did their best to support the strategies being trialled – like the time we came up with the playground bag idea – nearly everyone gave it a go and support grew for the bag as its role in reducing violence became apparent. It turned into one of our best ideas.

Our role as the playground team changed as time went by. At first, we concentrated on creating and maintaining our monitoring system. We wanted to know the nature of our playground problems so we could address them specifically. Our positive playground programme was fun to work on – raffles, mufti-days, equipment. I remember being excited as the data started coming in with lower levels of violence being recorded. Our ideas changed as we received feedback from teachers, parents and carers. Once, some parents expressed concern about one of our incentive programmes. Some teachers thought it would be good to reward the children who had kept the playground rules and did not appear in our playground book, for example, an end of term barbecue, or lunch with the headteacher, or a trip to the movies. Unfortunately, our plan seemed to have set up an 'in crowd' and an 'out crowd' mentality among the kids. Young children, children new to the school, and those with behaviour difficulties who were making progress, were all disadvantaged by our plan. Discussion was particularly lengthy as teachers argued that the prosocial children were not being acknowledged while others argued that the system we had put in place was unfair. We debated the issues of rewards and punishments and whether rewards should be given to children doing the right thing, especially those who usually don't – and whether allowance should be made for very young or new children at the school. We changed our strategy to avoid setting up an unintended hierarchy in the school community. It was good that the parents felt empowered and safe enough to bring this problem to our attention.

Gradually, teachers tried different classroom approaches to addressing violence and harassment. Our senior staff supported early intervention and the infants' teachers introduced social skills lessons into each class. The senior staff and I worked on delivering the targeted programme and by the second and third years, our monitoring system was firmly in place. We began to have more time to be proactive. Teachers were finding classroom programmes to teach social and emotional skills that they were comfortable to implement. With the targeted programmes in place, we were able to focus more on subgroups of children in the school, designing and trying different interventions. Our monitoring system allowed us to seek early intervention when it was clear that a child's difficulties were persistent.

I was a regular member of the team, seeding ideas from other schools, raising issues for debate and providing psychological perspectives. I set about finding remedial programmes and classroom lessons to try. Professional development came from various sources: visiting specialists, departmental experts, local learning and behaviour teams, educational psychologists.

Schools are busy places. That is why systematic approaches are needed to identify the nature and extent of violence for effective planning of the response. Supportive leadership, professional development, appropriate resources, support structures and communication networks are essential for the success of culture-changing improvement programmes. This is the time consuming yet valuable effort involved in designing and implementing change. When starting out, it is not essential, or possible, to design the 'definitive' response plan from beginning to end. As data is collected and analysed, interventions shift and change to match what is happening in the playground. Through a process of ongoing monitoring, evaluation and adjustment, a cycle of improvement evolves. Be aware that 'one-size-fits-all' approaches may miss the mark and may be expensive. In a review of such improvement models, Pogrow (2001) warns against embracing the 'bandwagon of comprehensive school wide reform models' rather than improving teaching quality and targeting interventions to specific year levels and individual student need. Instead, Pogrow supports the creation of local teams of experienced staff to provide ongoing support to schools. Local education authorities and governments clearly have responsibility to support early intervention programmes in this way.

Action Research

As schooling changes with new technologies and social changes, a new mentality of ongoing, active research is required. A flexible, goal oriented, ongoing approach to school improvement, called 'Ready-Fire-Aim', is espoused by Johnson (2001). Improvements are identified and prioritised and teams are selected to research and develop responses. The plans are then implemented, data collected and analysed, and an evaluation conducted. Adjustments are made and the new plan is implemented and monitored through an ongoing process of change. The cycle of flexible, data driven, ongoing action research ensures improvement continues.

'Ready':   designing a response plan: Accurate information about violence, rough play, teasing, bullying and harassment is collected to design a response plan. Observations, surveys, data collection sheets and interviews provide information from as many sources as possible, allowing an accurate measure of violence in the school. If violence levels are high, and it can be argued that zero tolerance of violence should be the standard, then immediate action is required and creating a violence response plan becomes a high priority. Decisions must be made to move the issue of violence up the list of priorities until it has been significantly reduced. Resources are directed to support the response plan, which is communicated clearly to students, teachers, parents and carers through as many forums as possible, for example, meetings with staff, parents, school assemblies, classroom discussions, newsletters, and the school handbook. Some schools will have to commit to long-term interventions, but there will be many short-term gains to celebrate along the way. If data analysis indicates that violence is not a big issue in the school, then intense levels of monitoring and policing are not necessary and staff can focus on universal, preventative programmes. Targeted programmes are still in place should children need extra help with their socio-emotional development. Answers to the following questions guide the development of a response plan:

- Is violence or harassment an issue in the school? Where is it occurring? Who is involved? What does the data show?
- Do headteachers, teachers and parents or carers lead children in respectful ways?
- Is a whole-school discipline policy in place?
- Do teachers practise research-based, effective teaching strategies?
- Are preventative programmes like socio-emotional development and peer leadership part of the mainstream school programme?
- Are strategies for monitoring inappropriate behaviour in place? Are data collection and management procedures simple to use?
- Have staff, parents or carers and children collaborated on the development of behaviour expectations, including rights, responsibilities and consequences?
- Are violence response plans clear and made known to all?
- Are targeted programmes available to children identified with socio-emotional skill deficits?
- Are parents or carers involved early when difficulties persist and supported in seeking advice from outside agencies?

'Fire': implementing effective interventions: Support structures are put in place around the response plan: a team is formed to monitor the programmes; staff are trained to deliver the primary and secondary level interventions; data collection and management procedures are explained; resources are found to support the response plan and parents or carers are kept informed and invited to contribute. A timeline is set out for implementation and evaluation of the plan.

'Aim': evaluation and refocus: Ongoing data collection, analysis and evaluation assists in deciding what has worked and what has to be refined or replaced. Strategies that prove effective are institutionalised and made part of the school culture. Response plans succeed or fail, depending on the level of ownership by the school, making ongoing discussion essential for change to be embraced by all stakeholders. Questions are asked about remaining challenges and the professional development needs of the staff, parents or carers and children. The process continues.

Support Structures

School leadership: Leaders emerge from all sectors of the school community but the ultimate position of leadership is the headteacher. Authentic school leaders represent the values of their society and have an opportunity to be agents of change, when required. Their leadership is knowledge based and the values they uphold build an atmosphere of trust and co-operation through mutual respect. Their personal qualities include social and emotional intelligence, enthusiasm, optimism, openness, flexibility and creativity. They are sensitive to others, politically aware and skilled in dealing with conflict. They reflect on their leadership style, guide the school in reflection on their values, attitude, motivations and challenge outmoded practice. They work with staff and parents or carers to identify the priorities of the school and develop response projects in an ongoing cycle of improvement. Their leadership style is flexible: coaching struggling staff; challenging the talented and listening to the concerns of the cautious. The steps of improvement projects are clearly set out and open for discussion. They aim to create professional educational communities through commitment to the following:

- ongoing improvement cycles of assessment, response, implementation, evaluation and refocusing of response
- professional development, time for ongoing reflection and planning, space and release from other duties for project teams
- organisation – communication systems, regular meetings, information boards, electronic mail, newsletters, suggestion boxes, questionnaires, induction booklets for new arrivals
- resources – provision of curriculum materials, teacher training days, LEA (district) resources, liaison with other schools, current research, access to other agencies
- flexible responses to ongoing feedback
- opportunities for the voices of all stakeholders to be heard, including children.

Senior staff structures: It is sometimes easy for the hierarchical structures of schools to disempower children, parents or carers and teachers, thus perpetuating a form of violence. Punishment, humiliation, ridicule and intimidation violate the rights of the child and lead to revenge cycles and distrust of adults. Senior teachers need respectful, democratic approaches when dealing with challenges in the school. Having said this, it is important for headteachers to act as adjudicators from time to time, having the final say when situations warrant decisive action. With headteachers in this judicial role, the network of teachers who deal with students in crisis are free to take a more supportive role, for example, act as 'emotional coaches' or mentors for children. Teachers dealing with children in crisis require a high level of emotional intelligence, that is, the ability to assess and take into account the emotional states of others, as well as their own. By viewing problems as teaching opportunities, teachers are able to guide children through the problem-solving process while supporting their emotional development. With reflection, mindfulness and training, it is possible to support a child in crisis with emotional first-aid while allowing natural and logical consequences to apply and providing children opportunities for growth and restitution.

An emphasis on emotional support does not reduce or replace the necessity for firm guidelines and consistent responses to violence. Behaviour standards, including rights, responsibilities and responses must be made clear and explicitly taught at school assemblies, in classrooms, at staff meetings and in school handbooks for parents or carers, making it easier for children to co-operate. It is still necessary for teachers and parents or carers to be strict on behaviour but permissive with feelings, allowing the adult to engage in the emotional world of the child.

Effective interventions: The most effective interventions into violence are integrated into the whole school and cater for different needs of children along a continuum of risk, ie, primary, secondary and tertiary levels of intervention (Walker et al, 1996). Primary level interventions are universal or school wide approaches are broadcast across the curriculum and across all ages and classes, with the aim of enhancing protective factors in all children. This is the most cost-effective level of intervention. The development of whole-school discipline programmes, effective teaching and learning strategies like making the curriculum interesting, maximising opportunities for success for each individual learner, teaching socio-emotional skills like anger management, conflict resolution and emotional literacy in the classroom, are all examples of primary level interventions (Walker et al, 1995). According to Reid (1993), the adjustment problems of 75 to 85 per cent of children are resolved with well-implemented primary prevention programmes. How important, valuable and achievable is this level of intervention!

Secondary level or targeted interventions address the insufficiencies of 'at risk' children. Small group lessons, behaviour contracts, emotional coaching, targeted programmes, counselling and mentoring are programmes that target children with identified difficulties. Sugai and Horner (1994) see effective targeted programmes as having:

- clear descriptions of difficult behaviours to address, for example Tommy fighting in the playground
- identification of behaviour triggers, for example Sam says things to annoy Tommy
- interventions that address behaviour triggers, for example intervention with Sam to eliminate teasing
- alternative behaviours defined and taught, for example Tommy attends lunch-time programme to learn anger management and help seeking strategies
- incentives and motivational systems in place, for example 'Congratulations' letter, time with mentor, external rewards
- long-term commit to monitoring, supporting, coaching, debriefing and teaching remedial programmes
- staff training and regular feedback, for example training in emotional first-aid, delivering targeted programmes, regular meetings
- systems for measuring and monitoring effectiveness are established for example, playground monitoring system, feedback.

Tertiary level or clinical interventions are required for children with persistent or severe, intractable problems that have not been modified through systematic primary and secondary level interventions. Collaborative, interagency approaches are initiated early to develop comprehensive, long-term interventions to involve parents or carers, teachers, peers, mental health clinics and social service agencies (Kukic, 1995). Tertiary level interventions are the most costly to society and must be delivered early in a child's life to be effective.

Playground teams: Teamwork helps share the load and creates the energy required to focus on the delivery of the response plan. When violence levels are high, this team may meet once or twice per week initially but reducing over time as the response plan begins to reduce the levels of violence in the school. Teams have a tremendous role to play on behalf of the school when violence levels are high, and in return should be given practical support, for example, time in lieu for the team leader, reduction in other duties, secretarial support, and a budget. Team leaders could be senior teachers who have remuneration packages to compensate the extra work involved. The role of these teams is to:

- lead discussion on violence and socio-emotional development with the school community
- research preventative and remedial programmes
- design a response plan with ongoing review
- monitor the playground programmes through data collection and analysis
- design positive playground programmes and incentives
- operate lunch-time programmes – for example, 'attention room', 'license to play', 'life space interviews'
- refer children to senior teachers and targeted programmes
- monitor individual progress – initiate interagency case management approach
- induct new families and teachers into the school wide response plan
- celebrate success.

Professional development: When violence is identified as a priority, professional development of staff and parents or carers is necessary to change the culture of the school. Staff need to be skilled in mediation, conflict resolution, emotional first-aid, mindfulness and reflection, and be able to teach socio-emotional skills across the school. Teachers need to have a clear understanding of the violence response plan to ensure consistency across the school. Teachers involved in an immediate response to violence need training in emotional coaching and life space interviewing. As priorities are identified, a time line for professional development is created. Schools with high levels of violence require high levels of support from local education authorities, the school community and government agencies. Training days and skilled support teams should be made available to these schools to provide ongoing support and development. Educational psychologists, learning and behaviour teams, publishing houses and other schools might also provide professional development.

Resources: There are a wide range of universal and targeted programmes available through publishing houses and some education authorities (see Chapter 17). Some school districts provide support teams to help schools access resources and training. Schools can help each other through cross-fertilisation of ideas and practical help with projects. Community service organisations also have an opportunity to support early intervention into children's lives in practical ways like funding school response programmes, donating resources and supporting fundraising projects. Schools must also find ways to provide teacher-time for implementing programmes. Someone has to type letters and response plans, photocopy data collection sheets, keep databases up to date, stock the playground bag and co-ordinate meetings. There are internal arrangements that schools can make to support the work of the team leader, for example, make the role part of a senior teacher's workload, or reduce other duties like playground supervision.

Parents or carers: Meaningful input from parents or carers is encouraged through invitations to join discussion groups at school; to send representatives to playground-team meetings; to help run positive playground programmes; to seek funding and resources from community service clubs and to support the school's response plan. Parent resource centres in schools provide a space for parents or carers to meet and support each other and provide a forum for other agencies to meet with parents or carers and schools. Educational programmes can be organised to meet the requests of parents or carers. The possibilities created by a well-functioning parent resource centre are limited only by people's time to meet and get organised. Communication networks between support agencies, parents or carers and schools are important when clinical interventions are required for children.

Section 2

Planting the Seeds – Proactive Programmes

Proactive Programmes

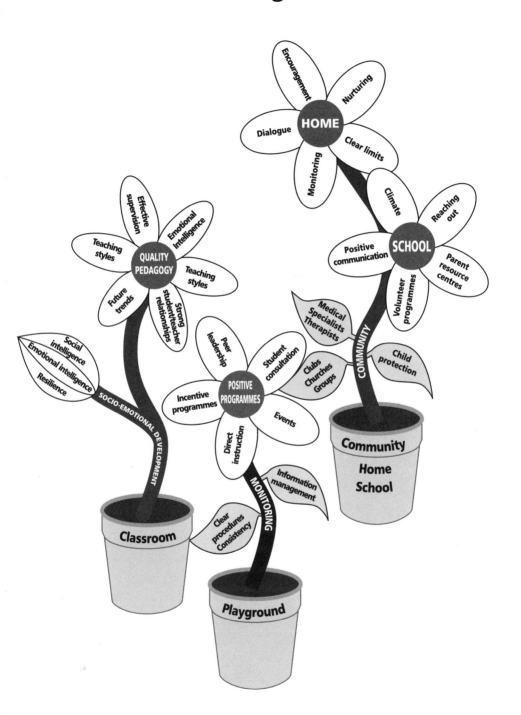

4

Classrooms

The story continues...

The teachers in our school were serious about the quality of their teaching. Regular professional development, organised by the senior staff, kept teaching style and content at an exemplary level. The teachers met frequently in their stage (year) levels to ensure continuity across the classes with an emphasis on the delivery of literacy and numeracy curricula. While there was a great deal of flexibility in the discipline and incentive programmes used in the classrooms, everyone used a similar approach to violence and aggression. Usually children were withdrawn from the classroom immediately and sent to a prearranged place, where they awaited an interview with a senior teacher. A simple recording system for classroom incidents was used that reflected the playground data collection-sheet. Over the years, we examined many classroom management and social skills programmes but each teacher adapted and used the systems that matched their own styles.

Gradually, teachers came to an understanding of the importance of socio-emotional development in the classroom – some more than others. The importance of teaching socio-emotional skills was becoming clearer, but the crowded curriculum in the upper years of primary school made it harder to include 'yet another thing' into the busy day. While the kindergarten to Grade 3 teachers took a systematic approach to teaching social skills, others were more likely to rely on the set physical education, health and personal development curriculum provided by the education department. At times, I was asked to find and model social skills lessons. Some of the commercial socio-emotional development programmes we came across had to be adapted to match our local culture, with changes in words, examples and amount of written work required.

We talked about emotional resilience and how schools can fill gaps in a child's support network. Sometimes a teacher is the only adult in a child's life with the resources or skills to show interest in their lives, preferences and interests. We may be the only adults in their lives who look for opportunities for them to grow and learn. Often teachers gave practical support to children – lunches, books, pencils, uniforms, first-aid…

Future Trends

Fundamentally, schooling is about student outcomes. Future thinkers like Hedley Beare, Professor Emeritus of Education, University of Melbourne, see the world as having moved out of the old paradigm of the Industrial Revolution era into a post-industrial world sometime in the mid 1970s. A new world-view has been forming and the agenda for contemporary education requires new patterns of thinking and acting that are radically different from what they were. Beare sees 'transformational learning' as being beyond provision of the 'useful information and tools' of the past. Students will increasingly bring critical faculties to the task of accessing information from a vast 'knowledge web', and from many different angles. He sees future educators as inspiring, creative teachers who are capable of transforming the learner with wonder and fascination, who are aware of the transcendent, who foster the magic of learning, and build a profound sense of responsibility in young learners. Beare describes transformational learning as:

> '...developing a reliable, enabling belief system; becoming a responsible citizen (which implies citizenship of the world and not merely of a single country); and growing a personal life-story which defines who you are and where your life is going.'
> (Beare, 2001, p18)

He sees intangibles like life purpose, aspiration and personal formation as making up a significant part of schooling, alongside the more analytical and traditional skills. Central to transformational learning is an attitude of life-long learning that develops the socio-emotional intelligence of teachers, parents, carers and students alike, along with thinking and learning.

Quality Pedagogy

At the core of school education is the classroom, with the enormous potential to produce, in tandem with parents, carers and communities, responsible citizens. Curriculum content is equal in importance only to the way in which it is taught and, in the case of socio-emotional development, the way it is lived. Teachers are central to schooling; their expertise and wellbeing pivotal to student outcomes. As a microcosm of the wider community, classrooms face the challenge of producing student outcomes that match curriculum objectives, while impacted upon by student, teacher, school, family and community variables. Teachers depend on life-long professional development to keep them up with informed understandings of teaching style, multiple intelligences, learning styles, reflective practice and action research. They need high levels of emotional intelligence manifested in positive relationships with students, collaborative approaches with peers and effective supervision.

Lifelong learning: The best teachers instill a desire to be lifelong learners in their students and are committed to the ongoing process of professional development. They are willing to review their teaching strategies and engage in reflection, action research and critical evaluation in order to adjust their teaching practice (Smith, 1993). They monitor their practice through mindfulness and reflection, peer review and supervision.

Teaching style: Teachers need a wide range of teaching styles to match the different learning styles and socio-emotional needs of their students. Concepts like multiple intelligences (Gardner, 1999), co-operative learning, mediated learning, transformational learning, democratic classrooms, and emotional intelligence should influence teaching practice in order to create positive classroom climates. The best teachers are motivational, inspirational, and excited about their teaching. They have excellent behaviour management and organisational skills. As intellectual leaders in their classrooms, teachers model critical thought and information processing skills. Their teaching styles increasingly reflect a future where information is readily accessible, diverse and subject to change over short periods of time. Flexibility in presentation and assessment forms part of a teacher's reflective practice. They routinely include lessons on self awareness, self control, empathy, listening, resolving conflicts, co-operation, values clarification and moral development.

Reflective practice and critical research: Giroux (1985) suggests teachers rethink their work by exploring the complexity of social relationships in the classroom, taking into account the social and historical peculiarities of the students with whom they work. As an example of this 'rethinking', Jordan (1997) describes using narrative and reflective practice as the teacher of a student with major behaviour difficulties who was resistant to learning. She examined her classroom practice through reflection and critical research and a reflective writing approach (Holly, 1989). She defined the challenge presented by the student and opened it up for discussion and debate among her peers and her students. She established a dialogue that considered both the student's, and her own view of reality. She held class discussions about power, relationships and choices. When Jordan considered the individual social, emotional and learning needs of the student she decided that the 'one size fits all' approach to discipline and learning was not suitable and changed her response. Individual guidelines and modified consequences were developed and discussed with the other students in the class who were, surprisingly, understanding and supportive of her proposals. She manipulated the curriculum content and her teaching styles to address the unique learning needs of this student while challenging, supporting and acknowledging the diverse learning needs of all students in her class. Her response was to expand opportunities for all. Jordan ensured the following key features were included in the planning, implementing and assessing of units of work:

- explicit teaching of all integral steps of a task to ensure clear understanding – multi-media, multi-sensorial presentations
- teacher and peer modelling of skills
- a range of individual, partner and small group tasks
- cross-age learning situations – peer tutors, buddy classes
- choices within a task that reflect preferred learning styles
- individual goals – targeted learning programs
- modified outcomes

- open-ended learning opportunities that challenge each student
- negotiated assessment expectations and timelines
- opportunities to share success in a variety of contexts
- negotiated presentation of assignments – a range of opportunities to demonstrate skills, knowledge and understandings, for example, not always having to write to show understanding
- relating the learning to students' own experiences
- ensuring students have access to support, for example, support teachers, peer support, mentors, emotional coaches
- making the learning a journey of discovery and fun for the teacher and students
- celebration of achievements.

Emotionally intelligent leaders: Emotional intelligence increases our ability to manage our relationships and ourselves effectively and, according to Goleman (2000), consists of four fundamental capabilities: self-awareness, self-management, social awareness and social skill. These are the basic skills we ought to teach to all children through words and actions, while increasing our own as we go. Goleman also applies these skills to leadership. As leaders in the classroom, teachers need a range of styles to manage a variety of situations and children, at times needing to be decisive, at others more visionary, or encouraging – moving back and forth between these styles of emotional engagement. Flexibility achieves the best results. Goleman's six types are:

Democratic – Consensus
- leader asks, 'What do you think?'
- builds consensus through participation, collaboration, fresh ideas, student input – not for use in a crisis.

Affiliative – Harmony
- leader says, 'People come first.'
- creates emotional bonds, flexible, empathic, communicative, healing, morale building – if overused can allow poor performance.

Authoritative – Visionary

- leader says, 'Come with me...'
- mobilises others towards a vision, clear direction, self-confidence building.

Coercive – Immediate compliance

- leader says, 'Do what I tell you to do.'
- used in a crisis, with a problematic class, to kick-start a project – used sparingly and with caution.

Coaching – Encouraging

- leader says, 'Try this.'
- empathic, goal setting to improve performance and develop strengths.

Pace setter – Excellence

- leader says, 'Do as I do – now.'
- sets high standards, conscientious, driven, self-directed projects – relative to each student.

Strong student-teacher relationships: Successful teaching relies on strong relationships between teachers and their students. Positive, caring and trustworthy relationships create classroom climates where children are open to the learning process. Create a positive classroom environment with rapport building strategies such as:

- Respect and honour yourself – live your values – make words and actions meet.
- Respect your students – honour their decisions, never use put-downs, give responsibility, enforce rules.
- Learn about your students – show interest in hobbies, sports, families, likes – find out what is important – understand their challenges and pressures – peer, academic, home.
- Acknowledge your students daily – say thankyou, use verbal praise, warm gestures, smile.
- Do special things – listen to their music, give a minute extra playtime, a 'no homework' week.

- Empower students – consult, value their input, give choice.
- Be open as a person – share your thoughts, ideas, challenges, experiences, feelings, values.

Socio-emotional Development in the Classroom

The overall message from preventative research is that schools can prevent the onset, severity and duration of problems like substance use, bullying, violence and mental health problems by creating a culture that promotes resilience in children (Fuller, 2001). Schools can provide many of the protective factors that support children's adaptation to difficult circumstances. Blum (2000) sees resilience as a comprehensive process, not programme, of establishing social support networks, teaching social, emotional, cognitive and academic skills, while creating opportunities for growth through participation. The adjustment problems of a majority of children are resolved with well-implemented school wide initiatives like teaching socio-emotional skills in the classroom or having positive playground programmes.

Unfortunately, social and emotional development vies with literacy and numeracy for a place in the curriculum of most schools, as though they were separate enterprises. As most teachers could attest, children need social skills and emotional management to co-operate with their peers in learning environments. One of the most time consuming tasks in some classrooms is helping children deal with interpersonal problems. Teachers can help develop children's social and emotional intelligences through formal lessons and by example.

Social intelligence: Social intelligence refers to the ability to read other people in social situations and to engage and interact with them to reach common goals. For social interactions to be successful, a range of skills are required, for example:

- social skills – turn taking, talking, listening, sharing, greeting, politeness, apologising, paying compliments, seeking help, joining in
- friendships – understanding the difference between being friendly and being friends

- communication – receptive and expressive language, assertiveness, reflective listening, explaining
- problem-solving – conflict resolution, mediation, conciliation, negotiating, accommodation.

Emotional intelligence: Emotional intelligence refers to the ability to read emotions in self and others and to manage these emotions so that cordial relationships develop. It includes motivation, zeal and persistence, and according to Goleman (1996), neurological data suggest that there is an opportunity for shaping children's emotional habits if we intervene early. Developing emotional intelligence involves:

- identifying emotions – body cues, words, actions, relating emotions to experiences, creating emotional vocabulary, labeling emotions
- self regulation – using self-calming strategies, self-talk, physical calming, problem-solving
- identifying emotions in others – observing body cues, words and actions, labeling emotion
- managing emotion in others – reflective listening, self-monitoring, clarifying, exploring, problem-solving
- healthy mind habits – thinking positively, being organised, being persistent
- using coping strategies- perspective taking, seeking help, cognitive behavioural approaches, desensitization, relaxation, fun.

Emotional resilience: Resilience refers to the internal and external adjustments we make when adapting to adversity and change. A protective social network for example, guards a child against victimisation, or the ill effects of a learning difficulty. Research into protective factors reveals a range of personal, family and peer/adult supports (Butler, 1997; Hawley & DeHaan, 1996; Walsh, 1996). followed a cohort of children over their lifetimes and identified the following factors in resilient children:

- personal/intrinsic factors – pleasant temperament, social intelligence, sense of belonging, sense of self-efficacy, high intelligence, a gift or talent, work success as an adolescent
- family factors – at least one warm relationship with a parent, a sense of belonging and connection, having qualities the family values
- peer / adult support – positive early school experiences, connection to school, achievement of academic goals, positive relationship with someone who believes in them

Positive relationships with adults create a sense of belonging and a secure base from which children deal with the challenges of life. For some children from chaotic backgrounds, this role can only be filled by a teacher, or some other member of the community. Children benefit from long-term involvement with adults, helping to develop their sense of identity. Adults act as role models of the 'honourable self' children are developing. Use social dilemmas to clarify values and promote moral development to encourage their growth as responsible citizens of the world. Skills like social and emotional intelligence, academic success and habits of thinking can be taught to children to help them develop a positive sense of themselves. Teachers have a direct role to play in this process of 'skilling' children for the challenges they will meet throughout their lives. Blum (2000) emphasises the importance of actively creating opportunities for children to practise and develop leadership, mediation skills, decision-making, humanitarian activities, responsibilities, adventures, fun, recreation and recognition of achievements. Set up peer programmes, take a class on an adventure trip, clean up around your block or visit a nursing home.

Teaching socio-emotional skills in the classroom: The importance of socio-emotional development in children is being increasingly recognised by its inclusion in personal development, physical education and health curricula. In an evaluation of 'The Resolving Conflict Creatively Programme' (RCCP), Roerdan (2001) reports that children who participated in this curriculum based instructional programme developed positively in terms of their world view, choice of non-violent conflict resolution approaches and non-acceptance of violence. Measures of academic performance also showed significant gains. The RCCP involved about 25 lessons per year focusing on socio-emotional skills like active listening, empathy, dealing with anger, perspective taking, co-operation, negotiation, appreciation of diversity and assertiveness training. As part of the programme, teachers received training and development on how to teach the programme. Administrative and support staff, as well as parents or carers, received training in conflict resolution and bias awareness. Peer mediators were trained and peer leadership encouraged. Schools implementing RCCP were asked to commit to at least four years of following the programme.

5

Positive Playground Programmes

The story continues...

We had a wonderful time working on the positive playground programmes. Occasionally, we joined with the grounds committee to design physical changes to the environment. Trees were planted, seats and tables put in place, areas for young children defined, sports areas designated, rosters for equipment created, games painted onto the playground and a covered sand pit installed – over a period of years. The raffle ticket system proved to be a great incentive and reinforcement programme. Again we debated about whether children who had been misbehaving should be given raffle tickets when they were found engaging in prosocial activities. Generally everyone supported handing out raffle tickets, some more than others. Kids loved it, and for six dollars a week – six ice-cream blocks from the canteen – we had heaps of children 'being caught' engaged in prosocial activities. One of the teachers sorted the raffle tickets every Monday morning to make sure someone from each year level was drawn from the lottery. Monday assembly had a real sense of fun and celebration about it. Another couple of successes were the playground box and the playground bag. The box proved to be a great way for children to seek help that wasn't urgent, as well as being the raffle ticket repository. Our work horse, the shoulder bag, held it all together. We kept the raffle tickets there, and plasters, cream, checklists and various other useful devices. We had lots of great ideas – fundraising days, talent quests, basketball competitions. Every little bit helped to make sure there was enough fun in the playground for everyone.

We had an active student representative council that was co-ordinated by one of the teachers. They organised events, contributed to discussions and passed up the concerns and needs of the student body. I was really impressed by the success of our peer leadership programmes. With supervision and support structures in place the programmes ran smoothly. I was closely involved with the peer mediation programme. Feedback from parents was positive; one mother told us about her daughter using her new-found skills at home with her sister. She was delighted! Her child found skills and confidence that stayed with her over the many years that I knew her. It seemed as if the kids matured as a result of the training and their experience. I noticed a definite reduction in my lunch-time programmes once the peer mediators were in operation. Not only were mediators helping to reduce the work by mediating for younger children, but interpersonal difficulties between these Year 5 and 6 children also reduced as they started using the strategies themselves. We talked a lot about whether any child could be trained as a mediator, with some teachers thinking that those who had been experiencing difficulties in the playground were not good role models for the others. We decided that they should be trained – the training would be of benefit to them – and we put in supervision and support structures around them. One of the best mediators I ever observed was a young man with whom I had spent many a lunch-time mediating between him and his friends or coaching him through his anger management skills. The mediators visited each class to explain how peer mediators helped kids solve their problems, where to find the referral forms and how to fill them in. Their contribution of time and dedication were acknowledged by the school.

Positive playground programmes ensure there is enough fun, freedom, resources and incentives to support children's play. Children need a free environment in which to practise their skills, create games, relax and 'do their own thing'. For many children the playground is the best part of school. This is their realm. This is where they plot, plan, organise and negotiate themselves into games. Play is the vehicle for learning that children naturally adopt and for the most part they do well. For others it is a complete mystery, or full of worries and aggression and these children are going to need help. Proactive programmes use a range of activities and structures to encourage prosocial behaviour while making sure the playground is a happy experience with as little interference from adults as possible. Following are examples of positive, proactive programmes and strategies:

- direct teaching of friendly playtime behaviour in the classroom, at assembly and in the school handbook

- incentive programmes to motivate children and reinforce positive behaviour – raffles, awards, celebrations
- student leadership through peer mediation, student councils, mentoring, peer referees
- student consultation about playground issues – the physical layout, play equipment
- adequate resources like play equipment, tables, stools, bins, playground markings
- events – sports, drama, dance, chess competitions run at lunch-time.

Direct Teaching

Classroom discussion: The rights and responsibilities of children in the playground need to be discussed frequently, with rules and consequences for anti-social behaviour need to be explicitly taught. Use social and moral dilemmas to consider alternatives to aggression and explore values. Lessons on emotional literacy, conflict resolution, anger management, alternatives to aggression, getting along with others, emotional resilience, values and moral development should be part of the mainstream curriculum.

Rule-of-the-week (or fortnight): The Rule-of-the-week is presented and explained at the general school assembly. Use role-plays or skits to help expand understanding of the rule and add interest to the assembly. The Rule-of-the-week is written up and displayed in the playground and classroom and discussed further during Circle Time or discussion time in class. The Rule-of-the-week can be reinforced through the playground raffle system. The rules can be made to match the behaviour challenges identified through the data monitoring system. Catchy phrases are used as 'scripts' or rule reminders, for example:

Hands off.	Play fair.
Keep it clean.	Be kind.
Take turns.	Take it when you're out.
Stop when the bell goes.	Invite others to play.
Play safe.	

School handbook: A school handbook is an excellent way to communicate with new parents or carers and families. As well as general information, details are included about playtime behaviour expectations and school responses, including parent involvement, when difficulties arise. Information about the positive playground programmes, how to contact staff when problems arise, the data collection system, and a description of targeted, remedial programmes can also be included.

Incentive Programmes

When using incentive programmes, take care to avoid creating a system that excludes or alienates children with difficulties and provides no hope of success. All children need to experience success and the progress of some children will need to be measured and celebrated against individual goals.

The playground raffle (lottery): A simple raffle ticket system can be used to shape playtime behaviour. Tickets are given to children observed in prosocial activities like helping others, picking up rubbish, organising games, playing happily and keeping the Rule-of-the-week. Specific feedback is given to reinforce behaviour while handing out the tickets, for example, 'Thanks for keeping the playground clean', 'Thanks for inviting others to play', 'Nice to see you playing safely', 'Good turn-taking'. Children write their names on the ticket and deposit them in the 'playground box'. Tickets are drawn at the weekly assembly and simple prizes are awarded, for example, frozen fruit juice, ice-cream, extra free time, an award or a canteen voucher. Tickets are given to any child observed keeping the rules, especially those with behaviour difficulties who are making an effort to change their behaviour or are caught engaging in prosocial activities. Some attempt should be made to ensure winners are drawn from each year level at assembly.

Citizenship awards: Children should be encouraged to value responsible citizenship through leadership programmes and school or community service. Citizenship is an important part of a child's development and ought to be included in student portfolios. Humanistic and environmental causes provide opportunities for children to contribute to the wellbeing of others. Certificates or awards may be given for activities such as:

- serving as peer mediators
- being buddies or mentors for new and young children
- training as a peer referee (acting as a referee for peers playing games like soccer, cricket)
- peer tutoring
- serving on the student representative council
- participating in community programmes, for example, visiting nursing homes, hospitals, carol singing
- school beautification projects – environmental care
- fundraising for charities or child sponsorship.

Whole-school celebrations: Celebrate whenever possible: violence-free weeks; clean playgrounds; accident-free weeks; achievements in sports, drama and debate. In fact, any excuse may be used as a cause of celebration. Celebrate through special announcements, letters home, pop-corn parties, extra playtime, ice-creams, barbecues, extra playtime, flags, posters, standing ovations, etc.. It is important to acknowledge and celebrate the progress schools make towards peaceful and happy playgrounds.

Student Leadership Programmes

Programmes are needed that create leadership opportunities for students in the school. Not only do they learn life-long skills through training for their roles, but they can also be a very effective tool in changing the culture of the school. When they work as mediators, referees, mentors, fund-raisers or any socially oriented role, they act as models to other children and reduce the amount of work for teachers. Students can learn simple leadership skills, for example: public speaking; acting confidently; being organised; working in teams; making decisions and taking responsibility (Grose, 2004). Children with highly developed social skills and emotional intelligence enjoy contributing to the school community when opportunities are provided to do so. Children have a way of relating to each other that eludes adults. The time and effort student leaders devote to their responsibilities, in turn, ought to be recognised and celebrated with citizenship awards, badges, hats, thanks etc. This wonderful resource can be tapped into with a little thought, creativity and dedication.

Student representative councils (SRC): SRCs provide children with a voice in school decisions and the chance to work for the good of their peers and the school community. SRCs, with the support of teachers, have the potential to develop leadership, organisational and teamwork skills in students. Representatives are elected from each class with positions held for a term to increase the chances of each student participating. Holding regular class meetings allows all students to raise issues for their representatives to present at SRC meetings, thus providing an experience of 'grass-roots' democracy. Confidence increases as the members of the SRC participate in a wide range of activities including:

- contributing to decisions about the school
- organising charity days, talent quests, sports contests, multicultural days, non-competitive sports days, grandparents days, art displays etc.
- being responsible for the playground box and peer mediation referrals
- making rosters for peer mediation, peer referees, equipment monitors
- organising games for younger children.

Peer mediation: Peer mediators are children who learn to help their peers resolve interpersonal conflict. By learning to treat others with respect, listen carefully, and referee when communication difficulties occur, they are able to guide their peers through a process that explores the problem, feelings and needs of the disputants and create options for solving the problem. Even young students can learn to guide peers through the problem-solving process. In a review of conflict resolution and peer mediation, Stomfay-Stitz (1994) reports a decrease in behaviour problems in the playground and a decrease in referrals to the headteacher. Students came to show greater respect for each other and staff spent less time serving as disciplinarians. Johnson et al (1992) studied the impact of a peer mediation programme on the management of conflict among students at an elementary school in Minnesota. Results were very positive with an eighty per cent reduction of student-to-student conflict referred to teachers.

Buddy or mentor systems: Students are trained to provide peer support to children new to the school. Buddies make sure their new 'charges' know where things are around the school, can find friends of their own age to play with and know how to seek help. Buddies might also be able, with training, to mentor children who are on targeted programmes, like the 'Passport to Play' (see Chapter 9) programme. Over time, contact is reduced but buddies tend to maintain special connections.

Peer referees: Children who are well accepted by their peers and have good social skills can be trained to act as peer referees and maintain order in games like cricket, basket ball, soccer, chess or other board games, without direct adult intervention. They are trained in the rules of the game, how to make a call or decision, being confident and assertive, applying emotional first-aid and when to call off a game. Local sporting identities or special guests can be invited to help train peer referees or visit the school to hand out certificates and add interest to the programme.

High school mentor programmes: Local high schools sometimes provide sports or academic mentors for primary school children, especially for those in their final year of primary school who might have difficulty adjusting to high school. Mentor programmes are sometimes conducted through high school courses like early childhood studies or physical education. Basic mentor training would be required.

Student Consultation

The voices of children should be heard; whether it is requests for help or suggestions they may have for management of the school. Their ideas are often creative and relevant and giving children a say about their school lives introduces them to the fundamental ideas of democracy and respect. Formal discussion or Circle Time allows a dialogue to grow that supports healthy attitudes and invites values clarification, moral development, tolerance and ethics. During Circle Time, opportunities arise for children to practise critical skills like presenting points of view, developing perspective, thinking critically, negotiating, problem-solving, creating options, self-management. The principles underlying Circle Time include unconditional acceptance without judgement or coercion and the opportunity to learn. In this forum it is safe for children to raise their concerns or ideas about their school. When each class has delegates on the student representative council, students have a voice in matters concerning their wellbeing.

The playground box: A playground box is a multi-purpose device that provides children with the opportunity to ask for help from a range of helpers in a formalised and confidential way. Referral slips and pencils attached to the box are used to contact helpers about playground issues. Helpers include peer mediators, school counsellors, the playground team, deputy, headteacher or volunteer teachers. Responsibility for processing the referrals can be given to peer leaders or the playground team. Referrals are passed on to the person nominated who then makes a time to meet with the child. The playground box also serves as a repository for the playground raffle tickets and a suggestion box. Children appreciate this opportunity to request help or make suggestions, especially in a large school where seeking help is sometimes difficult. Of course, more urgent requests for assistance should be made directly to teachers.

Playground Referral Sheet

Playground Help

Name: . . . .

Class: . . . .

Date: . . . .

Who Do You Wish to See?

● Peer mediators . . . . ☐

● Playground teacher . . . . ☐

● Headteacher . . . . ☐

● Deputy Head . . . . ☐

  'insert nominated helper's name' . . . . ☐

Resources to support positive playground programmes

Human resources: Intervening early in the cycle of violence through positive programmes prevents the entrenchment of aggressive response-sets in most children. Human resources are needed to monitor the playground and operate proactive and remedial programmes. Available personnel may include:

- local education authorities – specialist teams to consult about effective resources and programmes, provide staff training and long-term support

- school senior staff – leadership, active participation, support
- the playground team – design and monitor response plans, manage data collection
- teachers – support for intervention programmes, teamwork
- students – peer leadership programmes, prosocial models
- administration – typing letters, awards, entering playground data, printing off monitoring sheets
- community, parents or carers, sporting associations, high school students.

Physical resources for the playground: Physical resources are an important component of successful playground programmes. Problem areas that are identified through data collection can be addressed through close monitoring or physical changes designed to prevent violence occurring, for example, in hard to monitor places like corridors or behind buildings, in toilets. Children have many great ideas about making the playground more interesting and should be consulted about the physical layout of the school and the play equipment required. Resources include:

- play equipment: balls of all sizes, hoops, skipping ropes, passive games, basketball courts
- playground markings: snakes and ladders, checkers, hopscotch, handball, target practice courts
- large playground equipment: climbing frames, rope jungle-jims, sand play areas
- furnishings: tables, stools, quiet play areas, warm areas, shady areas, open spaces
- community resources: local playing fields, indoor courts.

Financial resources: Funding can be sought from education, health departments or community service-club grants. There is a role for government and community agencies in supplying the financial and human resources to address violence in our schools; after all, violence is an issue for the wider community and impacts on child development. When government and non-government agencies come to understand the role of early intervention in producing positive outcomes in children's lives, then we will see the proper allocation of resources to this issue. Small grants of money can make a big difference to school playgrounds, providing physical resources and equipment or training for students and teachers. In the meantime, schools are constantly on the lookout for grants of money. A useful document on how other communities have financed early childhood programmes, 'Making Dollars Follow Sense', may be found on the internet at http://www.nccp.org

Events, Games, Competitions

Talent quests, school plays, sports events, etc., provide interesting goals and projects for children to work towards. Community personalities and cultural groups can be invited to contribute skill development sessions, for example, ball handling, singing, dancing, playing chess. A theme for each term with scheduled events encourages co-operation among children and creates opportunities for the inclusion of social isolates in group activities. Possible events include:

- sports events – basketball competitions, soccer matches
- skill training sessions with community experts (sports, chess, dance, authors)
- talent quests
- chess days
- hobby days
- passive games days
- non-competitive games days
- mufti or fundraising days
- cake stalls
- loosely structured games
- sausage sizzles.

6

Home, School, Community

The story continues...

Our school was located in a fairly large town with a small hospital and some ancillary services. It was a tourist town, which meant there were lots of visitors passing through the town making it a very busy little cosmos. We were geographically discrete from other rural towns, which seemed to make us more interdependent as a community. Luckily for us, one of the workers in a community agency was conducting a pilot project that formalised interagency connections within the community. The project brought together community workers from the local council, health department, community services, schools, refuge workers, police liaison officers, drug and alcohol counsellors, church youth workers, etc. We met once a month to share resources, arrange professional development, talk about our services, co-ordinate programmes and develop interagency referral procedures. At the same time, the departments of education and health formalised the interactive nature of our work with a policy called School-Link. This policy supported interagency meetings making it possible for workers to mix across agencies, for example, speech and occupational therapists came to our school to conduct training and development sessions, to run therapy groups with children and to contribute to individual education plans for targeted children.

There was a high level of parental involvement at our school. The climate of the school was important to us. We made sure parents and carers felt welcome. From the administrative staff to the teachers and headteacher, all made sure visitors were addressed in a friendly and respectful manner. There was a suggestion box, comfortable chairs, reading matter and pamphlets in the foyer. Families were welcome at the whole-school assembly where they could watch the awards being handed out. Some of the school committees had parent representatives and there were a range of volunteer programmes for them to participate in. There were formal training sessions addressing literacy and numeracy and how help with homework and guest speakers were invited to talk on subjects of special interest.

Collaboration

The home, school and community are the substrate that supports the growth of a school community, through the common goal of enhancing student learning. The benefits of home-school partnerships, including enhanced academic learning, values, attitudes and skills have been described in numerous integrative literature reviews (Christenson et al, 1992). Successful collaboration is an attitude, not an activity. This attitude is reflected in relationships that treat all stakeholders as equals and has the goal of creating an ethos of learning in both home and school environments. It is felt in the atmosphere or climate of the school and develops through:

- sharing responsibility for a child's school performance – creating 'school-like' families and 'family-like' schools
- perspective-taking that allows understanding of the multiple demands on parents, carers and teachers that might limit their effectiveness
- clear communication – sharing the language of schooling, for example, grading and reporting practices and keeping home and school informed about each other
- keeping the child's academic success as the focus for home-school collaboration
- providing flexible opportunities for home-school collaboration.

On a broader level, societies that accept the notion that children are a social good and not a private burden will create the public policies to address not only parent education and early childhood care but also poverty, social exclusion and family-friendly workplaces. Edgar (2003), a social policy adviser, sees the way forward as having two aspects. Firstly, a new, more positive language of investing in children is needed. Rather than 'protection' and 'prevention' Edgar sees the importance of language that reflects the 'resourcing of families', 'promoting the positive' and 'surrounding and including' isolated or excluded families with supports for healthy child development. In this vein, the question is not 'Is the child ready for school?' but rather, 'Is the school ready to meet the learning needs of the child?' Secondly, he sees the need to build more responsive institutional forms at the local and regional level conveying the message that families are real partners in the process of making children part of the 'learning society'. New links between schools, parents, carers, community service agencies and businesses will open 'windows of opportunity' for the many children whose life chances at present are limited by their private circumstances and by outmoded public structures.

Thus, both the school and the home monitor students' progress and expect children to take responsibility for their learning and behaviour. The effectiveness of home-school collaboration is increased when programmes are tailor-made to fit the nature of the school, staff, parents, carers and community. Strategies must be culturally sensitive and planned at the school with substantial and sustained involvement of the headteacher, staff and parents or carers. 'Social capital', a term used by Robert Putnam, American social philosopher (Putnam, 2002), can be built through 'bonding' and 'bridging'. Bonding refers to relationships among people who are like each other: families, language and ethnic groups, religious groups or social identity. By respecting and drawing upon the cultures and communities they serve, schools are able to increase the bonding within their communities. Bridging, however, requires an attitude of tolerance and acceptance towards difference. Schools should make no distinction of religious faith or racial origin or socio-economic status. When children learn common principles, values and norms of justice and reasonable behaviour, they develop an understanding for different points of view, and the building blocks of trust across classes, religions, suburbs and cultures are developed. The critical role schools play in sustaining multi-cultural, democratic relationships is enhanced through easy, effective communication channels that develop mutual expectations of learning programmes, behaviour and discipline.

The Home Environment

Family influences: Families that have a sense of responsibility for their children's learning have a strong influence on their values, attitudes and behaviour. It is the skills and knowledge about how to help children's learning, rather than family status, that determines how successful children will be with their studies. Sharing information between home and school increases children's grades, and improves their attitudes towards school and their behaviour. Children are more engaged in homework activities and attendance is increased across all years and socio-economic levels of the families. Clarke (1983) in a study of home environments, differentiated what is called 'the curriculum of the home':

- frequent dialogue between parents or carers and children about learning and school, realistic expectations, post-secondary education
- strong parental encouragement of academic pursuits, recognition of effort and success, modelling of reading, study habits, persistence and completion of projects, mentoring, tutoring, provision of a learning space and resources (books, pens, dictionaries, etc.), visits to school
- warm and nurturing interactions, acceptance of children
- clear and consistent limits, similarity between home and school discipline and behaviour expectations
- monitoring of homework, TV watching, school attendance.

The School Environment

School climate: Positive climate building requires effort to reach out to parents or carers through a range of strategies, for example, having welcome signs, comfortable reception areas, displays of children's work, slogans, family fun nights, breakfasts, multicultural lunches, regular parent-teacher meetings, headteacher time for parents or carers, inductions for new parents or carers, school handbooks and positive school assemblies. Parents or carers are made to feel welcome and treated like VIPs. Conflict is resolved quickly and respectfully. The physical environment is attractive and reflects the pride that the community has in its school.

Reaching out to parents and carers: Often, it is not enough just to invite parents, carers and community members to be involved with events at the school. Coming to the school is easier if either a teacher or another parent makes a personal invitation. Some parents or carers may need extra support, for example, with transport, child care, translators or information presented in their primary language. Sensitivity to literacy levels is important when providing written information. Schools can provide support through information sessions, consultations, resources and frequent dialogue, thus increasing understanding of the language of schools and learning expectations. Parent-teacher conferences about student progress should be sensitive to parents' backgrounds with reports written in easy to understand language. Flexible arrangements can be made for parents or carers with work commitments that make it hard to attend meetings or events during school hours. Publicity about school programmes and events should be made through a variety or media including newsletters, flyers in local shops or libraries, parent networks and local newspapers. As soon as academic or behaviour problems are identified, parent-teacher conferences are called to identify goals and establish monitoring procedures.

The power of positive communication: When good things happen in a school, communicating this to the wider community improves the reputation of the school and increases goodwill. School-wide successes in academic, sporting, artistic and other arenas are broadcast to enhance the community feeling of the school. Good news phone calls are a great way to encourage two-way communication between home and school. Making contact when a child is not in trouble increases trust and co-operation between parents, carers and teachers. When children achieve goals or meet challenges, a phone call or written note encourages families, especially those with a child experiencing difficulties.

Parent resource centres: Parent resource centres can be set up to co-ordinate parenting resources like information and discussion groups, parenting books, videos, tapes and computers. Parent centres can provide information about children's learning, child development, parenting skills and other support agency networks. Expert visitors can be invited to talk about child development, helping with literacy and numeracy, social development, community services etc. Resource libraries of books, videos and tapes can be developed along with a range of pamphlets and handouts with tips for helping parents and carers with their children. Tea and coffee with a snack and time to share ideas with each other is a simple but effective starting point. The success of some very effective school-based parent centres is borne out by parents returning to education, improving their literacy and English-speaking skills or being empowered to seek employment. In some areas, parenting resources are linked to early intervention initiatives which provide co-ordination, and personnel support. Parent support groups need space and regular meeting times to grow and design programmes to meet the interests and challenges of parents and carers. Start with a survey of current parent requirements.

Parental input: Finding out about what parents, carers and students think is essential. Surveys, suggestion boxes, discussion forums and conversations between parents, carers and teachers helps create relevant curricula, school programmes and successful home-school collaboration. The more parents, carers and schools communicate about these issues, the more likely it is that relevant, local needs-based programmes are be developed.

Volunteer programmes: Parents and carers can provide support for a range of school projects, learning programmes or administrative tasks in the school. For example, volunteers can act as mentors to children with learning, social and behavioural difficulties, or extend the library hours for children. Celebration and recognition of parent and volunteer helpers builds the bonds that keep the school community thriving.

School committees: Schools operate many projects with which parents or carers could be involved, for example, antiviolence programmes, playground and environment committees, literacy development and parent and citizen committees. Parent participation in decision-making gives them a sense of ownership and belonging to the school community. In addition, collaboration communicates to teaching staff that they are partners with parents and carers in educating children.

Homework policies: Homework policies should be negotiated between teachers, parents and carers to develop a programme that is accepted and supported by all. Some thought should be given as to how homework can be made interactive, relevant and interesting, making it easier for parents or carers to help their children, especially in the early school years. Monitoring children's homework might have to be explained clearly to parents or carers through interviews, meetings or in the school handbook. To add meaning to a homework programme, teachers should check and reward children's efforts.

Community Environment

Community agencies: There is a wide range of agencies with a focus on child development available to support schools and families. Sometimes the roles and whereabouts of these agencies is hard for parents or carers to ascertain. Schools can establish communication networks with such agencies and provide parents and carers with information on services, venues and contact details. Local agencies usually include a variety of professionals and services, for example:

- general medical practitioners
- paediatricians
- child psychiatrists
- therapeutic services – speech, language, occupational, physiotherapy, counselling, family
- social security organisations
- child protection agencies
- police community liaison officers
- clubs – sports, services, community.

Collaboration with outside agencies: Within the community are many services and cultural organisations that can play a role in supporting schools with time and resources. Many organisations (solicitors' firms, university faculties, ethnic clubs) are beginning to consider ways of contributing to the social fabric of their country and can see the importance of supporting disadvantaged children. They could serve as mentors, donate raffle prizes, place paid advertisements in the school handbook or support ethnic celebrations. When these organisations are approached with a planned programme, that is simple but effective, they are more than willing to participate. Before and after school care programmes provide another way of supporting the social and skill development of children by using similar behaviour programmes or setting up mentoring, tutoring and homework projects. Fetes, fairs or information nights can be held to bring together the range of community resources available to provide support for families

7

Monitoring The Playground

The story continues...

This strategy worked really well for us. It started with us creating a hierarchy of behaviour problems to ensure we all knew what we meant by the various terms being used. We talked extensively about terms like violence, bullying, teasing and harassment. We came up with operational definitions for physical, verbal, and social or emotional violence, rough play and temper outbursts. We decided that all of these behaviours were serious enough to warrant an interview.

It took a lot of commitment to keep the records up to date – collecting the checklists from the bag, entering the information into the playground book and doing the statistics by hand. Once administrative assistance was made available, data was entered into a computer database and the statistics were easy to obtain. The headteacher took a great interest in generating statistics, which allowed us to target specific groups of children. For example, when the data showed that many children were recorded as playing out-of-bounds, we started a campaign of instruction and reminders at assembly and in class. We made sure that the induction process for new children included a walk around the playground with the out-of-bounds areas pointed out. On another occasion, it became apparent that there was a lot of rough play recorded against a particular group of Year 5 boys. We responded with discussion about safe play at assembly and in class. Several teachers, including the head, volunteered to take this group to a nearby oval every second day where there was more space for them to play games like soccer and cricket. This took the pressure off the whole playground, making more space available to those left in the school.

Our playground bag evolved into an integrated part of our monitoring system. It contained the data collection sheets, raffle tickets, a first-aid kit, emergency disc for summoning help, behaviour and response hierarchy, photos of children with medical conditions that might need emergency care – in fact, anything that might help the supervision of the playground. The emergency disc was a laminated red cardboard disc with an 'E' printed on it. If the playground teacher needed quick emergency assistance with a situation, the emergency disc was given to a child to summon help from other teachers. It meant that in intense moments, the teacher on the spot did not have to rely on children to explain that extra help was needed. Other teachers offered immediate support when a child brought in an emergency disc. Teachers also kept a disc in their classroom. We used a shoulder bag with a front pocket for easy access to the raffle tickets that we were 'sprinkling liberally'. Casual teachers loved the bag; it made playground supervision much easier for them. Most teachers used the playground bag when they were on duty, entering data, handing out raffle tickets, but not every teacher complied – a few chose not to use this resource and in a spirit of tolerance towards individual preference, no-one was forced to comply. This did not seem to matter in the end – we were obtaining enough information to help us target our resources. As the value of the process became more obvious, the practice became more widely used.

The playground monitoring system was invaluable to my role in the school. I was in the school for one and a half days per week, which made it hard to keep up with what was happening in the playground. The playground team kept the records up to date and entered incidents alphabetically into a book, making it easy for me to look up children's names and monitor their progress. While the senior teachers dealt with each act of violence immediately, it was my role to deliver socio-emotional development programmes to these targeted children, usually at lunch-time. The playground team also made sure I received the data collection sheets recording specific incidents of violence for me to follow-up. Collecting data and keeping statistics was crucial to monitoring the playground and targeting resources. Also, it was encouraging when we saw the recorded incidents of violence reducing.

It is easy to overlook the importance of collecting data and keeping records, especially in busy schools where it can seem like just one more thing competing with the many important tasks needing to be done. However, collecting data makes it possible to target resources to problem areas, monitor the progress of individual children and evaluate intervention strategies. Each school is different. In large schools or schools with high levels of violence and harassment, data collection is essential to gaining and maintaining control of the playground. Vigilance and persistence is needed until a system of social and emotional support is established and an ethos of harmonious relationships with ongoing improvement is achieved. On the other hand, small schools or schools with little violence may decide to keep simple records. Whatever the circumstance, collecting data and maintaining records is good professional practice, guiding our response plans and supporting our celebrations of progress. To monitor the playground effectively, schools need clear procedures that are understood by all, simple data management systems and mechanisms for reporting success to the school community.

Clear Procedures

To ensure consistency of teacher reporting and to make sure children are treated fairly and consistently, teachers must understand not only what is involved in data collection, but why it is important. Discussion and debate about playtime behaviour and responses to inappropriate behaviour is important and leads to clear procedures and shared understandings. Different models work in different schools, so trial and adjustment will develop an approach that teachers can support.

Hierarchy of inappropriate behaviour and responses: Following is an example of a hierarchy of inappropriate behaviours and responses that was developed in consultation with teachers, parents and carers to reflect local values and circumstances. Terms and procedures were debated until consensus was reached, resulting in a widely supported list of misbehaviours and a range of responses. Bullying, teasing and harassment will need to be discussed at a whole staff meeting to ensure everyone knows what they are observing and recording. This hierarchy guide lists behaviours at four levels of increasingly serious behaviours. On the right hand side of the hierarchy, a range of responses is listed for teachers to apply when dealing with each level of misbehaviour. Teachers had plenty of latitude to make judgements about individual situations, using whichever of the responses on the right hand side they thought best. However, everyone was asked to treat acts of violence seriously by following the agreed strategy of immediate withdrawal and an interview with a senior teacher and recording the details of the incident on the data collection sheet. A copy of the hierarchy can be reduced in size, laminated and placed in the playground bag for quick reference. This strategy provides an easy way for casual teachers to access the information they need to supervise the playground.

Inappropriate Behaviour – Response Hierarchy

Behaviours	Range of responses
Level 1 Playing out of bounds Playing without hat	**Level 1** Interview with playground teacher Rule reminder
Level 2 Disobey teacher Rough play Loss of temper Teasing Swearing	**Level 2** Incident recorded Interview with playground teacher Time out Referral to targeted programme
Level 3 Ongoing harassment Bullying Violence Repeated Level 2 behaviour Fighting Verbal abuse	**Level 3** Immediate withdrawal, interview Incident recorded Parent contact Referral to targeted programme Referral to educational psychologist
Level 4 Serious physical harm Repeated aggression Repeated Level 3 behaviour	**Level 4** Immediate withdrawal, interview Incident recorded Parent contact Interagency response Individual management plan

Information Management

Information from direct observation, surveys of students, teachers, parents, carers, serious incident reports, suspension records, referrals to targeted programmes etc. can be used to track the progress of the school's violence response plan. Teachers are more likely to comply with data collection when they see the value of the process, when it is simple to use and when it does not take their attention away from supervising the playground for too long.

Data collection: A quick and easy-to-use data collection device is required for recording information from the playground. When inappropriate behaviour is observed, the behaviour level is identified from the hierarchy, responses are chosen and a data collection sheet is completed. Following is an example of a 'quick-tick' data collection sheet that records valuable information from the playground:

Data Collection Sheet

Date.................... Teacher...

Name(s) of those involved   Year

....

....

....

....

☐ Rough play   ☐ Swearing

☐ Teasing   ☐ Bullying

☐ Fighting   ☐ Violence

☐ Disobeying Teacher ☐ Other

Further details...

....

☐ Follow-up required

Playground bag: The playground bag holds tools for monitoring the playground and provides easy access to procedures, data collection and incentives. A bag is especially useful during the intense phase of implementing improvement plans, or in large schools. Bags are kept centrally for processing of data sheets and stocking with resources, for example, in the staff room or office. Things to include in the playground bag:

- data collection sheets
- behaviour-response hierarchy
- red emergency disc to summons immediate assistance
- profiles of special needs children (medical, emotional, behavioural difficulties) reduced and laminated – include the child's details, management plan and photo – useful for big schools and casual teachers
- 'Playground referral' sheets (also attached to the playground box)
- peer mediation rosters
- raffle tickets for the playground incentive programme
- simple first-aid kit – tissues, plasters, rubber gloves, antiseptic cream
- pencil, sharpener, pens.

Databases: Information from data sheets is entered into an indexed book or computer database. Databases provide easy access for monitoring individual progress, referring children to targeted programmes, sending home positive letters, giving playground awards, celebrating success and contacting parents or carers when violence occurs or when there are repeated, less urgent breaches of playtime behaviour codes (playing out of bounds, temper, rough play, disobedience). Suggested headings:

Date	Name	Year	Incident	Teacher	Follow-up

Data analysis: Simple percentages, graphs and frequency distributions provide enough information to guide the school's response plan and support good news broadcasts. This task should not be onerous and may not always be necessary. When playground data is analysed, patterns of behaviour problems emerge and may be used to guide the allocation of resources. For example, it may be found that the younger children are wandering into other children's games. In response, a supported play programme could be designed to help younger children develop game-playing skills and playground awareness. Peer leaders can be co-opted to work with younger children on passive and active games, helping to get games going and acting as referees. On the basis of data analysis, teachers may decide to set up specific programmes such as an attention room or a passive play area.

Feedback: Opportunity should be created for reporting back to students, teachers, parents or carers about progress in playtime behaviour management. Progress buoys the spirits and strengthens efforts towards planting a culture of peace. Celebrations add a positive atmosphere to the school and act to bind communities together through shared successes.

Section 3

Tending the Garden – Response Strategies

Response Strategies

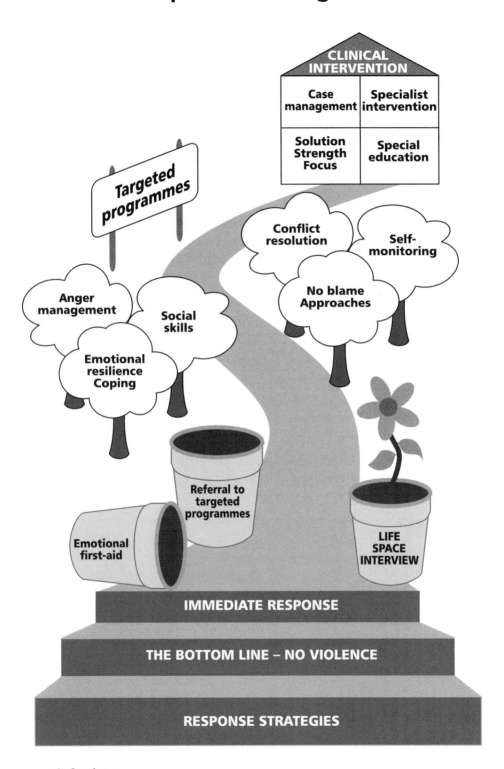

CLINICAL INTERVENTION

Case management	Specialist intervention
Solution Strength Focus	Special education

Targeted programmes

Conflict resolution

Self-monitoring

Anger management

Social skills

No blame Approaches

Emotional resilience Coping

Referral to targeted programmes

Emotional first-aid

LIFE SPACE INTERVIEW

IMMEDIATE RESPONSE

THE BOTTOM LINE – NO VIOLENCE

RESPONSE STRATEGIES

8

Immediate Response

The story continues...

We all agreed we needed a response to violence that involved immediate attention – withdrawal from the playground to a designated 'cool off' place – an interview with a senior teacher. Teachers dealing with crises became skilled in lowering the emotional temperature and 'slowing things down' – allowing time and space for children to calm themselves down before working through the problem. We knew which children had emotional and behavioural difficulties and put in supports around them, for example, individual management plans, buddies, emotional first-aid, teacher's aides, anger management training and friendship skills lessons.

My personal interest was teasing, harassment and bullying. Over the seven years, I interviewed hundreds of children using a brief, solution-focused, blame and shame free interview strategy that worked in almost every situation (see Chapter 9). If it didn't work, we quickly invited parents to help work on the issues with us. An environment where children tease each other, relentlessly, can easily get out of control. When left unaddressed, a cycle of hurt and shame develops, leading to anger and violence with sometimes devastating results, as sadly witnessed in recent times. Children respond well to respectful and unbiased attention that leads to meaningful assistance. After talking to so many kids, I realised a few things. Most kids have been teased and lots shrug it off. But those who experience hurt or shame need to have the teasing 'turned off' and to learn some of the things the resilient kids do to manage teasing. Another thing I learnt was that most of the kids engaged in teasing are 'pests' – when approached in the right way they usually stop, especially if you keep checking. Many feel real remorse and empathy grows. The children who continue to tease need a higher level of monitoring, for example the 'Passport to Play' programme (Chapter 9). Another thing I have learnt is that some children – often the 'bullies' – cannot handle the assault to their self-worth they experience when teased and fall quickly into a shame-anger cycle. Anger management training is only half of the story. We also need to turn the teasing off. This can be a BIG job. I had to negotiate with my school about not taking referrals for certain other work while I focused on addressing teasing immediately using a blame-free interview strategy. It worked beautifully – but it needed commitment of time to interviewing and following up – time well spent when the culture among the kids began to change. This valuable role should be built into someone's job description – it needs a time allocation, part of the 'attention room' idea perhaps.

At first things were hectic. On particularly busy days, kids sometimes had to wait on the verandah or until the next break or the next day for their interview. Of course, the more serious incidents were dealt with immediately. The playground team and the senior staff, with support from the whole school, carried a heavy load for quite a while, but the effort paid off as more and more children came to the understanding that they would have to account for the choices they had made when resolving interpersonal problems. Having a response plan that included immediate withdrawal from the playground and referrals to targeted lunch-time programmes, meant teachers knew what they were doing and children's needs were being met.

Violence is not acceptable in the school community. There are many reasons for it, and it is widespread, but schools that focus on the issue and persist in working constructively will reduce the incidence and acceptability of violent and aggressive acts. The terms 'violence' and 'aggression' used here refer, in general terms, to the emotional, social or physical harming of others or destruction of property but ought to be defined operationally at each school. The ideas suggested in this chapter refer to violence in the playground but, in principle, also apply to violence in the classroom. The formula is simple: teach personal development skills including Emotional Literacy and social skills throughout the school; be firm on the bottom line of 'No Violence'; support the school's violence response plan, including immediate withdrawal, emotional first-aid, interview and referral to targeted programmes and refer children for further intervention when they do not respond to these measures. Children who do not respond to universal and targeted programmes require intense support through a case management model which includes educational psychologists, specialist teachers, parents, carers, other agency specialists and where necessary, special education settings.

When Violence Occurs

Physical violence and aggression: A consistent response that includes immediate withdrawal from the playground, emotional first-aid as needed, an interview with a senior or 'crisis intervention' teacher and contact with parents or carers is required. This response to violence is made known throughout the school community and is applied consistently and persistently to every incidence of violence. Opportunities for learning occur at these crisis points through constructive adult response to children's behaviour. Within an atmosphere of harmony, possibility and co-operation, children learn about self-regulation, the reactions of others, responsibility, problem-solving, consequences, and restitution. At these crisis points, staff members are needed who are skilled in emotional coaching, crisis intervention, mediation and no-blame approaches to work calmly with upset children. With emotional support and skill development, children can be empowered to take responsibility for their actions. When we take the time to listen and help children reflect on what has happened, we develop an understanding of the motives and values behind their actions. Their trust in adults increases, adding to their store of emotional resilience.

Violence occurs within social contexts and teachers usually know the histories of children who act violently. These children will benefit from having a mentor who can act as an emotional coach (for example, senior teacher, counsellor, educational psychologist, helping professional or community volunteer) to help them gain the skills of emotional control, co-operation and problem-solving. While a lack of emotional control is not behind every act of violence, immediate withdrawal, emotional first-aid as needed and an interview, no matter what the cause, helps children realise that violence is not acceptable and that they will have to give account of their actions, explore alternatives to aggression and consider acts of restitution every time.

In general, an immediate response to physical violence includes:

- securing the safety of all children – summoning extra help as needed (red emergency disc), separating aggressors, dispersing onlookers
- applying both physical and emotional first-aid as needed
- gathering the basic facts for an incident report
- withdrawing violent children from the playground immediately – sending or escorting them to the pre-arranged 'chill out' area to wait for an interview
- using child-safe methods of restraint but only as a last resort.

Bullying, teasing and social exclusion: Bullying is commonly defined as a form of aggressive behaviour in which there is an imbalance of power favouring the perpetrator. It is unjustified, repeated and experienced as oppressive by the target. Teasing can have an element of fun about it, but if it is mean-spirited, then it is likely to have similar effects on the target as bullying. In some ways, these forms of violence are harder to observe and therefore manage. Targets tend not to report these incidents, unless specific measures are taken in the school that encourage disclosure. Despite the covert nature of this form of violence, the results can be devastating to the wellbeing of targets who can carry the scars into adulthood. When left unassisted, targets can become perpetrators of violence themselves as a perpetuation of the 'shame-anger' cycle. Teasing and bullying are seriously detrimental to positive school cultures and deserve an immediate response. When harassment has been identified, immediate support is provided for the target. Perpetrators are interviewed using strategies that are solution focused, provide opportunities for restitution, do not focus on blame and guilt and avoid shame, for example, *The No Blame Approach* (Maines & Robinson, 1997). Most children respond to these approaches and cease their harassment. For a few, prolonged monitoring, mentoring and parent assistance may be required.

Disclosure of harassment can be encouraged through school wide approaches that inform students of their rights to come to school without being harassed and informs them of their responsibility to treat each other with respect. Gradually, the culture of 'not telling' can shift by reframing the reporting of teasing as 'seeking help'. Another problem is that teachers sometimes ignore requests for help with teasing, either because they think kids should deal with it themselves, or more often than not, they are truly too busy to be of assistance. Schools should appoint key personnel to manage the response to harassment and let parents, carers and students know who these people are and how they can be contacted. Much persistence is needed to reduce harassment significantly in the school. Each case must be followed up religiously. Targets of teasing can be taught a range of ways to manage being teased, making them more resilient and 'immune' to teasing.

Crisis Intervention

Teacher values, attitudes and skills: To successfully guide children in crisis through a set of predictable steps while ensuring opportunities for problem-solving, goal setting, skill development and restitution teachers need particular skills and attitudes:

- respect – neutrality, fairness, concern for human dignity, respectful language
- empathy through understanding of emotional disturbance, violence, child development and medical conditions like Asperger's syndrome, Autism
- optimism – confidence in children's abilities to build up their social and emotional skills
- ability to model calmness, emotional control and problem-solving skills
- consistent responses from staff are that predictable and well known to staff, children and parents
- emotional coaching and emotional first-aid – acknowledgment of the physical and cognitive components of emotions
- Life-Space Interviews – emotional control, values clarification, problem-solving, goal setting, skill development and restitution
- the ability to mediate between disputants
- blame and shame free approaches to children
- solution-focused approaches that provide opportunities for children to make restitution for their actions.

Life Space Interview (LSI): The LSI is a verbal technique for working with children in emotional crisis developed by Fritz Reidl (1966) while working in an institution for emotionally disordered youth and expanded by Nicholas Long et al (1991). LSI provides emotional support through constructive adult responses to the events surrounding a crisis thus expanding a child's understanding of their strengths, values, behaviour and the responses of others. They are immediate (after emotions have subsided), meaningful, solution-focused and aim to create the empathy and emotional space needed for restitution to occur. The aim is to empower children to take responsibility for their actions, increase self-regulation, empathy and problem-solving skills and develop their trust in adults. By finding the values underlying a child's actions, one is able to join with their view of the world and help build a positive response to the incident. Identification of values is a crucial step in the interview. Values are the gold within children that dissipates guilt, shame anger and revenge cycles when acknowledged, leaving the way open for solution-focused approaches. The motives of most children are usually based on good values, such as defending their own or another's honour, confronting what they see as unfairness, avoiding hurt and shame and having fun. The difficulties start for the child when they choose antisocial approaches to meet these 'noble' ends. Once co-operation has been gained, children are usually able to identify positive alternatives for solving their problem. Children need a few basic skills to engage in a LSI:

- ability to describe events
- ability to listen
- minimal understanding of words
- basic reasoning skills
- trust in adults.

Life Space Interviews have the potential to provide mediated learning experiences for children solving interpersonal problems. According to Feuerstein (1980), individuals have the potential to change and are 'modifiable' if provided with the opportunities to engage in the right kind of interactions. This may seem like a time consuming process, but children learn that while violence is not tolerated, they will be assisted in finding alternatives to aggression. Through this process, respect is modelled and a sense of confidence in the child's ability to resolve problems without violence is created. Of course, the school responses are still implemented, for example, joining an anger management group, and opportunities for restitution are provided.

LSIs occur close to the time of an emotional crisis. If a child is emotionally distressed, it will be necessary to lower the emotional temperature by applying emotional first-aid until the child is able to talk about the incident. Chapter 14 uses script to illustrate fully the stages of a LSI. Briefly, the steps are:

1. Establish an empathic connection – use reflective listening, positive self-talk, scripts and emotional first-aid until the child starts talking about the incident.
2. Focus on the incident – ask questions, clarify, reflect back, understand.
3. Identify the values, strengths and central issues for the child – establish therapeutic goals – protect dignity, show respect.
4. Use solution focused problem-solving approaches – brainstorm options, evaluate, identify consequences and acts of restitution, choose plan.
5. Plan for success – rehearse, anticipate the reactions of others, accept consequences for actions.
6. Re-enter normal activities – calm, matter of fact, responsible.

In general, it is judicious for the Life Space Interview to be conducted by a senior or nominated teacher rather than the headteacher, allowing the teacher to refer to the headteacher's confidence in children's ability to resolve their differences in friendly and polite ways. This intermediate step puts children on notice and encourages them to take responsibility for meeting their challenges in prosocial ways. Failure to do so would mean an interview with the headteacher and parents or carers, thus providing the child with extra motivation for co-operating. Follow-up with the headteacher is essential when a Life Space Interview is not successful.

Emotional first-aid: Sometimes we minimise the emotional needs of children by expecting them to function effectively in a crisis, at a time when they have little control over their responses. Emotional first-aid recognises that emotions are based on physiological reactions involving the biomolecular systems of the body (Pert, 1999). As such, they have a course to run, sometimes taking up to 20 minutes to return to 'normal'. Children can learn to identify their body's early warning signs of emotional distress and to pause, or slow down the process enough to intervene through physical and cognitive means. As children calm down, they start to use more rational words to talk about their experience. Physical symptoms reduce and agitated activity calms down. When they are ready, they can then engage in a Life Space Interview. It may be necessary to apply emotional first-aid again during the interview as the child copes with issues that are raised. If they do not have sufficient emotional control after 20 or 30 minutes, it may be necessary to address the issue at some other time. For further details on emotional first-aid, see Chapter 15.

Restitution: While a school's responses to violence must be immediate, moderate and connect logically or naturally to the incident, it should also meet the socio-emotional development needs of the child. For example, when children act violently in the playground, immediate withdrawal allows them to calm down and ensures the safety of others and is a logical consequence. Referral to a remedial programme to learn alternatives to aggression is also logical. Care must be taken to avoid punishments since they generally lead to cycles of resentment and revenge. Children need more guided practice of the skills they are learning rather than lengthy isolation from the playground and their peers. Restitution refers to the process whereby children take responsibility for their actions by acknowledging the harm caused to others and by finding a way of repairing any damage to property or relationship. Restitution is an important way to build relationships and improve children's self-concept. When there is a chance to make amends, children are able to develop empathy for the target and can develop a view of themselves as someone who is able to think about problems and come up with solutions. This face-saving device releases the child from the futile grip of guilt, giving them the psychological space to understand the repercussions of their actions. Children are encouraged, not forced to engage in acts of restitution and can choose what to do in consultation with the target, if deemed appropriate. Acts as simple as apologising are acceptable, as are offers of help to fix things, written letters of apology, agreeing to attend targeted programmes, stopping other children from teasing or seeking help for their interpersonal problems.

9

Targeted Programmes

The story continues...

Our systematic approach to identifying children in need of extra attention meant we were better able to provide targeted, remedial programmes. The success of these programmes really depended on having support structures in place for those of us who worked through lunch-times to deliver the interventions. Resources had to be found and communication channels set up. A lot of the programmes were run at lunch-time and my office became an 'attention room' of sorts where children were engaged in a range of activities designed to teach specific skills. Lunch-time proved a very effective time to run the programmes. Children were investing some of their own time in gaining new skills and discipline problem problems were not a big issue. They seemed to learn really quickly at lunch-time, especially when they knew they might have to return to finish the programme in the next break. It was important to keep the programmes brief and solution-focused. Targets of teasing were invited to play games designed to develop emotional resilience and assertiveness, but not necessarily at lunch-times. At times, I acted as an emotional coach. I recall working with an eight year old boy on anger management. We talked about anger, its physical aspects and how he felt about it. We worked out where he first felt anger in his body and what were his best 'chill out' strategies – he preferred to be left alone for about five minutes to regain emotional control. We devised a plan – if his body told him he was becoming angry, he would ask to sit alone, without anyone talking to him, for about five minutes. This plan was shared with the staff and worked really well. After he had gained control, he was ready to engage in a Life Space Interview.

Children targeted for remedial work fell into three categories:

1) Young children and those new to the school who didn't know the rules or expectations of the playground.

2) Children who were often on the periphery of fights or bullying, who were silly or annoying and easily influenced.

3) Children who were often in trouble for violence. Most children in the first two groups responded to our interventions, suggesting that when they were given clear instruction, limits and targeted, remedial attention they were able to change their behaviour.

The statistics I kept on the targeted lunch-time programme showed that over a year, most kids – fifty-two of the ninety children referred – were only referred once. Twenty-six of the ninety had between two and five incidents recorded. Eight of the ninety children referred had six or more acts of violence recorded against them. Only four out of the ninety children referred needed an intense case management style of intervention. Children in this third group tended to have clinical reasons for being aggressive, including conduct disorders, autistic spectrum disorders or victims of abuse including domestic violence. In these cases, home, school and community services were accessed to build support networks around these children. Our results were encouraging and gave us the confidence to continue supporting such an intense response to violence and aggression.

I had negotiated my role in the school so I could support the lunch-time programmes. I found everything I could about socio-emotional skills – getting along, empathy, anger management, mediation, resilience, self-monitoring. I made sure lunch-time programmes were interesting and non-punitive and included role-plays, therapeutic board games, puppetry, fun and laughter. At first, the volume of work felt enormous. I took my lunch break at a different time and sometimes interviewed children during class time. Anyone with high emotional intelligence can run targeted programmes, with professional development in how social learning occurs and how targeted, remedial programmes work.

Support Structures, Skills, Strategies and Resources

Targeted or remedial programmes are early intervention strategies that provide structured learning experiences that focus on specific socio-emotional skills for small groups of children identified as needing extra tuition. Targeted programmes work best as brief, solution-focused interventions that include fun activities and are delivered by adults with respectful, neutral and fair attitudes. Most children learn prosocial ways to solve interpersonal problems from their social environments at home, school and the wider community. However, for some children extra tuition through targeted interventions is needed in small group settings. Placing children into targeted programmes allows differentiation between children with serious emotional or behavioural disorders who will need clinical interventions and those who have gaps in their socio-emotional development, for whatever reason. Children who have gaps in their learning usually apply the skills they have learnt from targeted programmes to future interpersonal problems while the small minority of children who have more serious disorders will need individual case management plans.

The philosophy behind running targeted programmes at lunch-time is one of support and attention rather than reprimand and detention. Care must be taken to avoid a sense of punishment that often leads to cycles of revenge. No-blame, curious and respectful attitudes create a supportive environment for solution focused and strength-based interventions to occur. Targeted programmes work particularly well when children are required to invest some of their lunch-time to attend the programmes. The cost-benefit dynamic of the lunch-time approach provides children with an added incentive to apply their new skills. Children are released from the programmes as soon as they show they have learnt a range of alternative behaviours to use and understand what is required of them in the playground. Repeat offenders are monitored closely. Through persistence in monitoring the playground and responding consistently, including referral to targeted programmes, children are encouraged to take responsibility for their behaviour.

Staff running targeted programmes at lunch-time need support in the form of resources (fun programmes, attendance books, pencils, incentives) time-in-lieu, and a room or designated area. They also need professional development in Emotional Literacy, social learning and modelling, crisis intervention, mediation and conflict resolution.

The attention room or chill out room: The concept of an attention room or chill out room is a positive slant on the more traditional detention room approach used by many schools for playground problems. Attention rooms are open at lunch-time and playtimes and function as the main venue for dealing with playground difficulties. Space is required for resources like tables and chairs, chill-out areas, access to water, and space for teachers to conduct Life Space Interviews, therapeutic games and small group lessons etc. Depending on the level of violence and harassment in the playground, a number of teachers and senior staff, aided by peer leaders or mediators, are required to operate the attention room. The attention room provides a range of services and resources:

- a designated area to which children with playground difficulties are sent
- Life Space Interviews with individual children
- therapeutic games with groups of children – friendship skills, emotional resilience, anger management, playground issues, personal development
- skill-reminder worksheets – anger management, hands-off, friendships, problem-solving
- mediation for children in conflict provided by peer or teacher mediators
- chill out areas for children needing time and space to calm down
- access to water as a calming strategy
- a base for peer support and mentoring programmes
- problem-solving and planning sheets
- posters of playground rules
- self-monitoring programmes like 'Passport to Play' – children meet in the attention room at the beginning of each play period for 'pre-correction' sessions, ie. they revise their goals for playtime or their anger management plan.

The fluctuating nature of playground problems means staff need to be flexible in their approach to operating an attention room. Records of attendance are kept to ensure repeat offenders are carefully monitored to enable referrals to tertiary level or clinical interventions are implemented when necessary. Letters are sent to parents or carers when children attend targeted programmes and to acknowledge improvement. Attendance in the chill out room is brief and solution-focused.

Emotional coaching: Emotional coaching is a strategy that can be used by senior teachers, trained teachers, SENCOs or community mentors when working with children who have ongoing emotional difficulties. Emotional coaches meet with their students or mentees for half an hour once a week to guide them through the process of gaining emotional control, finding coping mechanisms and consequently, increasing their emotional resilience. Coaches are emotionally intelligent adults who believe in the importance of relationship and are dependable, persistent and respectful role models in the child's world. They are able to read the emotions of others while recognising and dealing with their own emotions. They look for opportunities to expand children's social and emotional skills. They teach and use emotional first-aid when necessary and conduct Life Space Interviews to help children negotiate their way through interpersonal crises in ways that encourage responsibility and restitution. While empathising with children's feelings and motives, they support the limits placed around their behaviour, allowing natural and logical consequences to occur. They demonstrate empathy through reflective listening, eye-contact, verbally supportive statements and non-judgemental attitudes towards the child. Coaches use a range of strategies, including the following:

- At a calm time, the concept of emotional first-aid is discussed with the child. Children are interested in hearing about their body's physiological responses to anger. This understanding helps them see anger as something they can manage, making them more likely to use calming strategies.
- Teach children to identify their body's early warning signals, for example, tight fists, chest, shoulders or throat, feelings in the stomach, legs or head.
- Teach the child a range of anger management skills, including physical, thinking and communication skills.
- Help children identify the emotional control strategies that work for them.

- Assist the child to set goals for emotional and behavioural control.
- Discuss what might happen if they fail to develop emotional control.
- Teach positive self-talk that reflects 'calm' and 'control' and identifies the child's strengths
- Create optimism through recognition of success – encourage persistence.
- Use the steps of a life space interview when necessary – apply emotional first-aid, talk about what happened, identify feelings and values underlying the behaviour, talk about self-control strategies tried, give behaviour specific feedback, set goals.
- Review progress regularly, reset goals, reinforce success with rewards – awards, stickers, specific verbal praise.
- Work with parents, carers and teachers – inform them about the child's successes and the anger control strategies being tried – obtain accurate feedback about how the child is going in other settings.

Therapeutic games: Therapeutic games provide a fun way of teaching socio-emotional skills like getting along, solving problems, empathy, resilience, friendship, anger management and self-monitoring. Children identified with socio-emotional deficits can benefit from playing therapeutic games. Games are highly motivating to children, making them a great vehicle for targeted, remedial programmes and ideal to include in lunch-time programmes. Therapeutic board games have key concepts imbedded on the board-face or on cards turned over during the game. Challenges or dilemmas are presented for children to resolve using the key concepts of the game, with a good dose of fun and chance built-in. Games can be used in the classroom to support emotional literacy curricula, or in the 'attention room' with targeted children, or as clinical interventions with individual children.

As well as being a useful teaching tool, the experience of playing a game with a skilled game leader provides an opportunity for mediated learning experiences to take place. Interpersonal difficulties that arise during a game allows the leader to guide children towards prosocial ways of resolving problems. Brief Life Space Interviews during a game helps diffuse crises and provide valuable teaching opportunities. During a game, leaders guide the discussion and teach new skills while modelling co-operation, respect and teamwork. Discipline problems are minimal when the games are played on 'kid-time', that is, break or lunch-time. As much as the games are fun, most children would rather be out playing with their friends and will usually co-operate to avoid having to come back during the next break. If a child is particularly disruptive and does not respond to Life Space Interviews or appeals for co-operation, then playing therapeutic games in groups is not likely to be an effective strategy for this child at this time. Children who have not responded positively after about six to eight sessions are likely to require more intensive, clinical intervention involving home, school and community agencies.

Other resources: Many commercial programmes and resources are available to teach social and emotional skills with fun worksheets, videos and activities that motivate and inform children (see Chapter 17). Having fun experiences enhances learning and every effort should be made to find interesting ways of teaching socio-emotional skills to small groups of children. Care must be taken to match the literacy levels of the child with avoidance of worksheets that could frustrate children with learning difficulties. Children co-operate with the programmes and are more likely to learn and apply new skills when it is targeted at their level and it is fun or interesting.

Remedial Programmes – Socio-emotional Development

Modelling, coaching, behaviour rehearsal and social reinforcement are central to the success of remedial programmes. Small group work on social skills lessons, appropriate worksheets, therapeutic games and other commercially available resources provide the opportunity for children to practise new skills. Section 4 outlines a range of 'tools' of culture change. From experience it appears that the most common socio-emotional skill deficits observed in the playground include:

- poor social and friendship skills
- conflict and poor problem-solving-skills

- low emotional resilience
- inadequate anger management
- poor self-monitoring skills.

Social and friendship skills: Children with social skill deficits benefit from guided practice in basic skills like turn-taking, talking, listening, using manners, sharing, negotiating, explaining, working in groups, impulse control, apologising, accommodating, making restitution and so on. These social skills are best modelled to children incidentally while working with them. Children who have been identified with social skill and friendship difficulties can benefit from small group, direct teaching of these skills. Exploring friendships, friendliness and politeness releases children from some of the angst associated with being 'told' to be friends with everyone. Not all children like each other and preferences for friendships ought be respected. The difference between being 'friends' and being 'friendly' is an important concept for children to understand. Children should not be expected to be 'friends' with everyone at school, they have a responsibility to be 'polite' at least, and hopefully 'friendly' with other children. When they understand this difference they are usually more likely to include others in their games since they do not have to be 'friends' to play together or co-operate in the classroom. Children who continue to be mean to others will need to be reminded about school policies and the responsibility they have to be polite and the role their parents and headteacher have in helping them meet this responsibility.

Conflict resolution and mediation: Mediation is a respectful way of helping people in conflict communicate and co-operate to resolve interpersonal problems. Schools can provide a mediation service through both peer and teacher mediation. Mediators guide communication by asking questions; helping to create options; acting as referees and ensuring respectful communication occurs between disputants. Skills include: reflective listening, assertiveness, a win–win attitude, emotional control, critical thinking, and empathy. Mediators are neutral, confidential and respectful. They do not act as police officers and do not tell children what they should do to solve problems. Training children to be peer mediators gives them lifelong skills, empowering them to resolve conflict and solve problems. In this way, an ethos of co-operation and persistence in the face of conflict is created in the school.

Both teachers and peers are able to act as mediators for children. A study by Zhang (1994) in a New York school showed that training teachers and administrators in conflict resolution enhanced students' interpersonal relationships. The advantages of training staff include minimal disruption to daily school routines, high teacher motivation, long-term duration of the training effects and reduced financial burden on the school. Many minor conflicts dissipate with early intervention by a teacher acting as a mediator who uses problem-solving steps to resolve conflict. The process of mediation is not difficult, especially when working with children, but it does require commitment to neutrality, confidentiality and fairness.

Following is a basic structure for conflict resolution. Chapter 12 has a fuller description of the mediation steps.

- Ask questions – define the problem.
- Ask about feelings, fears or concerns.
- Talk about the needs of the disputants.
- Brainstorm options.
- Evaluate options by considering the consequences and possibility of each option.
- Choose solutions agreeable to all parties.
- Make a plan.

Teasing and harassment: Adopting non-judgemental, respectful approaches to teasing and harassment encourages empathy in perpetrators while exploring acts of restitution. By avoiding the issue of blame and guilt, children avoid being shamed and are encouraged to take responsibility for their actions and make plans for how they can make school better for the target. *The No-Blame Approach* (Maines & Robinson, 1997) is an excellent example of this type of approach.

A brief, solution-focused approach to teasing was developed by the author to work with the large volume of students engaged in teasing and harassment. This brief interview approach proved highly successful in reducing teasing very quickly. In this model, perpetrators are interviewed individually with targets given the option of attending. During the interview, a series of simple questions that focus on honesty, empathy and restitution are presented. The situation is closely monitored and a follow-up interview is conducted a week later. Follow-up is essential to ensure harassment has ceased. All children involved with the teasing must be identified and interviewed. If harassment does not cease, the problem will have to be resolved between the headteacher, student and parents or carers.

Following is an example of a brief, solution-focused, blame free interview. Interviews last between five and fifteen minutes.

Preamble: A general statement is made indicating that teasing and harassment are not accepted at the school and that the headteacher would like to give those involved a chance to solve the problem themselves. If they cannot make a plan, then an interview would be arranged with the headteacher and their parents or carers.

Phase one: The aim of this phase is to gain admission of involvement in the harassment. Statements of fact are made, for example:

- 'I understand that you are one of the children involved in calling X names.'
- 'I have been told that you sometimes make school hard for X.'

Most children admit involvement with very little prompting when the interviewee remains neutral and makes a statement of fact. When children hesitate to admit involvement, offer to interview witnesses to the harassment. Sometimes children say they used to do it but have stopped now. Thank them and proceed to phase two of the interview. If children claim to have been harassed by the target (or anyone else), offer to help them with the problem at the end of the interview.

Phase two: the aim of this phase is to increase empathy for the target. Examples of questions include:

- 'Have you ever been teased?'
- 'How did you feel?'
- 'How do you think X has been feeling?'

Most children are able to say that they did not like being teased and that the target would be feeling bad, mad or sad about it. Some children really don't care about being teased and seem to shrug it off. If children are not able or willing to state how they think the target is feeling, make a statement about how you have felt when teased, for example, 'I felt like I wasn't as good as others when I was teased'.

Phase three: The aim of this phase is to help the perpetrator to think of ways to make school better for the target. Examples of questions include:

- 'What could you do to make school better for X?'
- 'What could you do to solve this problem?'

Most children will at least say they will stop. Others will offer to apologise, or tell others to stop. These suggestions are accepted and recorded. If children are unable to think of anything to do, then let them know what other children have thought of doing. If children are unwilling to think of anything to do, then offers to contact parents or carers or the headteacher to help them think of ways to fix the problem.

At the end of the interview, let children know that you will inform the headteacher about their plan and that you will be checking with targets to make sure harassment has stopped. Also, state that you will see them in a week's time to see how well they are sticking to their plan. If they had mentioned they were being teased, ask if they would like your help. Teachers also need to support targets by setting up monitoring and reporting mechanisms. Targets usually benefit from exploring strategies for dealing with teasing, for example, through therapeutic games. Persistence in following up incidents of teasing and harassment is crucial to eliminating these problems from the playground.

Resiliency and coping skills: Children develop emotional resilience when there are social support networks around them and when they develop a range of strategies for coping with their problems. When working with targets of teasing, it is important to tell them of their right to attend school without being teased or harassed. Explore their feelings and thoughts about being teased and help identify adults they could approach if they need help. Help-seeking needs to be normalised in schools and sanctioned by adults. If teachers are approached by a child, then they must offer help or arrange for another teacher to assist the child. This is a very important step in changing a culture where getting help is seen as a weakness and often discouraged by adults.

Teacher 'help' is also an important feature of training children to be more assertive and to 'stick up for themselves'. Children who are timid need to know who they can be assertive with and who they cannot. Perpetrators of teasing generally fall into two categories: 'bullies' who victimise others by saying or doing unpleasant things; and 'pests' who generally go along with a bully or are just silly and annoying. Bullies usually do not stop unless adults intervene but pests will usually stop when asked to by children. Characterising perpetrators as pests or bullies helps children decide whether to be assertive with a pest by telling them to stop annoying or to get help from an adult when being harassed by a bully. Different responses are explored, including humorous sayings that might be used to lighten up the situation when being teased by a pest. The difference between being funny and being mean or sarcastic is also explored.

Using therapeutic games allows a child to practise new-found skills like assertiveness, help seeking and ignoring without getting into a worse situation. Having fun while playing games with a group of friends and a game leader also desensitises them to teasing.

Anger management: Children can learn strategies for managing anger at quite young ages, in fact the earlier, the better the chance of shaping the brain's biomolecular response to frustration and anger. Children can learn a range of physical, cognitive, communication and lifestyle skills to help them handle anger. Self-calming ideas are explored like talking sense to oneself, going somewhere quiet, having a drink of water, getting help from adults. They can learn to apply emotional first-aid by identifying their body's early warning signs and creating the time and space to calm themselves down. Assigning an emotional coach to work with a child will help them identify their early warning signs and create a list of strategies for calming their emotional response, debrief them after a crisis and monitor and celebrate their progress.

Teachers, parents and carers can help children calm down by allowing them the time and space to settle before working through problems together. Teaching anger management skills can introduce a range of calming strategies while exploring alternatives to aggressive behaviour. The difference between being assertive and being aggressive can be explored. The main teaching points would include:

- We all feel angry sometimes but it is not OK to hurt anyone.
- We can catch anger early by listening to our bodies.
- Stop when you first feel angry – give yourself time and space.
- We can think about what to do when we feel angry.
- Sometimes we need to take a break when we first feel angry, for example, get a drink of water, take a walk, sit somewhere quiet and think.
- Ask for time out if you need it.
- We are assertive when we stand straight and tall, look the person in the eyes and say what we want to happen.
- We are being aggressive when we hit, shout, kick, punch, pinch, scream, threaten.
- We can solve problems together when we calm down and take time to think.
- Tell yourself 'calm down', 'I can work things out'.
- It's OK to ask for help when we need it.

Self-monitoring – Passport to Play: Children who are learning to monitor their own behaviour sometimes need structures and supports in place to remind them of their goals and reinforce their successes. A brief interaction with a teacher before play and a physical reminder – a passport with their personal goals listed – can help a child develop their own self-monitoring skills. The Passport is a card or small booklet containing the child's details and behaviour targets. It can be personalised with the school logo and decorated by the child. To further the analogy with a passport, it could contain details like hair and eye colour, age and date of birth. Behaviour targets are specific and matched to personal goals and stated simply, for example, 'Hands Off', 'Ask for help', 'Take it when you're out', 'Walk away', 'Have a drink of water', 'Calm down', 'Play carefully'. The Passport programme is meant to be a brief intervention to help children learn to monitor their own behaviour. A Passport can be used when:

- close monitoring of children with anger management difficulties is required
- pre-correction or rule-reminders are needed before a child enters the playground
- children have a coach or mentor support for goal setting, debriefing, encouragement
- short periods of supported play with a teacher, aide or peer leader are required
- limits to free play time are needed – behaviour is monitored from a distance and play time is gradually extended.

For example, if a child has been attending anger management lessons and has progressed enough to re-enter the playground, a self-monitoring system in the form of a 'Passport to Play' can support the child's reintegration. Before playing, the child would collect their passport from their teacher who briefly reminds them of their target behaviours, for example, 'get help if someone annoys you' or 'hands off'. At this 'pre-correction' session, they could also revise their anger management plan. At the end of playtime they return their passport to their teacher who briefly discusses the play session with the child, offering congratulations and encouragement. Following is a sample Passport. Ticks are placed in the squares after each play session as children meet their targets:

Passport to Play

School
logo

Name: ....

Class: ....

Date of birth: ....

Date of passport: ....

Hair colour: ....

Eye colour: ....

Target 1   Hands off ....

....

☐☐☐☐☐☐☐☐☐☐☐☐☐☐☐

Target 2   Ask for help.................................

....

☐☐☐☐☐☐☐☐☐☐☐☐☐☐☐

Target 3   Take it when you are out

in a game ....

....

☐☐☐☐☐☐☐☐☐☐☐☐☐☐☐

10

Clinical Intervention

The story continues...

Over the years, our statistics revealed that about one or two per cent of the school population needed a clinical level of intervention. This meant that in our school of 600 children, there were generally about six to ten or so who needed individual programmes and outside agency involvement per year. Because of our systematic monitoring and consistent response plans, these children were identified early in their school experience. These are the children who do not acquire socio-emotional skills from their homes, the classroom or targeted programmes. A range of other educational specialists may also have been consulted, for example, behaviour specialists, learning teachers, educational psychologists. Some of these children had been assessed through the community health system and diagnosed with syndromes like Asperger's syndrome, Autism, Tourette's syndrome. Some were diagnosed with mental health disorders like Conduct Disorder, Opposition Defiant Disorder, depression or anxiety. Others had experienced abusive home environments. Some had intellectual delays or learning difficulties while others were reacting strongly to teasing. For one or two children, no explanation was found.

When children with disabilities or behaviour disorders had been identified, a case management approach was activated and a working team established. Team members included different people at different times, for example, parents, carers, teachers, child psychiatrists, clinical psychologists, social workers and doctors and sometimes the child. Case management meetings provided a broad view of the child and ensured all learning, medical, therapeutic and family support mechanisms were in place. Through this consultative process, intervention programmes were devised, monitored and revised as needed. Programmes ranged from full-time adult supervision through behaviour training with specialist teachers to ongoing mentoring and counselling. We were able to keep most of these children in the mainstream setting and with adequate supervision and support for the child, teachers, parents and carers, the safety of the other children was assured. On one or two occasions, a child was placed in a special education setting. In a way it didn't help that there were so few special education services in our area, but in another way, we had to do it ourselves. We had to create a supportive, calm, respectful, fun environment for everyone. Teachers really needed solid support with appropriate teaching styles, individual education plans, teacher assistants, and emergency procedures in place.

Clinical intervention is costly and time consuming and often the last avenue of support, all the more reason for early intervention. Most children who reach this level of involvement will have been through a range of interventions and families will most likely be distressed. If a child has not responded positively to the systematic social skill training and positive behaviour approaches in place at the school, then investigation of organic syndromes, medical disorders, family dynamics, child protection issues etc. is the next step. Consultation, assessment and ongoing involvement with professionals like child psychiatrists, clinical psychologists, paediatricians, physiotherapists, occupational, language and counselling therapists may be required to gain a broader picture of the child. At times, agencies like health, housing, social security and community services might also be involved, identifying and addressing disadvantage and distress, while helping families build resources. Alternative programmes and options are needed that keep these children engaged with the schooling process for as long as possible, that directly teach coping strategies, develop functional skills in social, academic, and behavioural domains and that provide respite for at-risk students and the regular school placement setting (McMillan et al, 1996, Walker et al, 1996).

Attitudes

Positive school cultures are welcoming and supportive of parents or carers and are essential for developing the relationship of trust that allows collaboration when challenges emerge. Proactive schools have bridges and bonds in place with families and support agencies that make working together that much easier. Schools are a pivotal agency for bringing other agencies together to meet the needs of the child. In a future time, as public policy, interest and support for early intervention increases, children will arrive at school with a multi-agency support team working with parents or carers to ameliorate disadvantage. In the meantime, children often turn up at school aged five, without prior intervention and schools are left with the task of identifying challenges and designing interventions under difficult circumstances.

When problems are persistent, respectful, strengths-based approaches help families identify their resources and minimise dependence while providing practical assistance. In a climate of trust, most parents or carers are open to seeking support to meet the challenges provided by their children. When working across agencies, parents or carers' wishes should be respected; informed consent gained and active participation encouraged. Respectful interactions are characterised by:

- friendly, positive and confidential communication between families, support agencies and the school
- two-way communication that ensures parents and carers understand the 'special' languages used by health and education professionals
- non-hierarchical structures and equality of stakeholders
- strengths-based dialogues about the challenges being faced
- an understanding of child development and the perspective of the child
- solution-focused versus deficit models
- holistic views of the child
- culturally sensitive interventions.

Strengths-based approach: Families, parents, carers, children and communities possess a range of strengths that determine the vulnerability or resilience of a child. Strengths-based research identifies seven strengths that fortify the resilience of families:

- communication – talking, listening keeping communication channels open
- togetherness – a sense of belonging

- sharing activity – family rituals, outings, fun
- support – physical and emotional assistance
- affection – eye contact, touching, hugging
- acceptance – acknowledging and accepting each other's strengths and weaknesses
- commitment – being there for each other in all circumstances.

A family's potential for repair and growth is affirmed when dialogues between agencies and families turn problems and deficits into challenges and opportunities for growth. Focusing on strengths allows attention to shift from deficits to assets on which collaborative relationships and effective interventions are built (Saleebey, 1992; DeChillo, 1996).

Inter-agency collaboration: Working collaboratively across agencies is a well intended and well worn cliché that is often lost in the translation to busy, under-resourced agencies and families. Scott (1993) examined the question of effective inter-agency collaboration in the context of organisational constraints. Collaboration involves complex organisational, personal and professional transactions. She warns against lapsing into a state of powerlessness that can lead to burnout and a high turnover of workers, stressing that it is at the level of the individual worker that we can work towards effective collaboration. Suggestions include:

- Recognise that inter-agency conflict is structural not personal. Acknowledge different organisational interests.
- Build goodwill at the interpersonal level by creating opportunities for informal contact and positive social interaction.
- Build goodwill at an interagency level by developing interagency protocols, organising joint information days or seminars.
- Avoid making other agencies the enemy.
- Use solution-focused approaches when dealing with conflict.
- Form coalitions with other agencies on the broader agenda of policy change and improvement of services.

- Build a knowledge-base of effective collaboration strategies by examining what is happening elsewhere, for example, journals, conferences, other districts.

Interventions

When children have not responded to proactive and targeted interventions, a team of caseworkers, including key stakeholders like the parents, carers, child, teacher and other agencies is formed, and a range of interventions considered:

- medical intervention, child psychiatrists and paediatricians, medication (with close monitoring)
- therapeutic intervention – speech therapy, physiotherapy, occupational therapy, counselling, family therapy, parenting courses
- specialist behaviour consultation for children with syndromes or disorders – social stories, visual programmes, individual behaviour programmes devised to meet the specific needs of the child
- intense academic, social and emotional skill development
- mentoring, emotional coaching
- supported play, adult supervision – 'Passport to Play'
- special education placement – the least restrictive setting should be considered
- support agencies like – community health, child protection, housing, employment, non-government organisation.

Case Management

Case management is pivotal to the success of clinical interventions and outcomes for children. A case management approach allows interventions to be monitored and refocused as necessary. A case manager is appointed from the lead agency involved with the child and family, although it can be hard to identify the lead agency in complex situations. While the lead agency is often the school, care must be taken not to overload school staff with this responsibility. Case managers are responsible for:

- co-ordinating agendas and meeting arrangements
- mediating between stakeholders, including the child
- acting as an advocate for the child, representing the perspectives and needs of the child
- ensuring strengths-based, solution-focused approaches are used to set learning goals
- ongoing monitoring and evaluation strategies
- keeping team members informed about progress and celebrating success.

Solution-focused Interview

Non-judgemental, positive approaches where the strengths and competencies of the child and family and child are foremost work best. Keeping the focus on creating learning goals is especially important when families are disenfranchised or uninvolved. A conversational, comfortable style of interaction that avoids emotion, blame and sadness establishes rapport and keeps communication open. Positive language that expresses concerns as learning goals encourages families to develop a view of competence and increase motivation to change. According to Durant (1995), 'problems' exist only in language. Thus, 'problematic situations' are reframed as 'challenges' and 'problems' defined in solvable ways. Parents and carers have a wealth of skills and strengths, both known and unknown to build upon. Rather than focusing on the deficits and weaknesses of the situation, a focus on strengths and resources helps orient families towards success. When families have a say in the process of change and their preferences are respected, they are more willing to co-operate with the case management process. In a solution-focused approach:

- The focus of the meeting is the child's academic, social and emotional performance, including successes, strengths and needs.
- Discussion centres on what the school wants to teach the child, not on the child's deficits. Concerns are presented as learning goals.
- Specific, observable language is used to describe the child's performance or behaviour.

- Options are explored for reaching goals. Brainstorm ideas without evaluation until everyone has had a chance to contribute.
- Ideas are considered, evaluated and prioritised.
- One or two options are chosen that consider the strengths of the child and family to meet goals.
- Roles and responsibilities are assigned.
- Parents or carers are invited to assist and asked about their preferred way of helping.
- Practical assistance is provided to meet identified family deficits – food, housing, daycare, transport, parenting, homework.
- Monitoring procedures are in place with a time frame for evaluation of the plan. Ongoing adjustments are made.
- Successes are celebrated.

Special Education

When concerted, but unsuccessful efforts have been made to implement socio-emotional and behavioural programmes aimed at supporting children with difficulties in mainstream schools, the disruption to the learning of others has to be considered. Evidence is mounting that combinations of syndromes, head injuries and child abuse lead to brain dysfunction, that is, something physically wrong that impedes the ability to play by the rules of society (Gladwell, 1997). In chronic situations, the biomolecular system in young brains becomes programmed to response-sets of agitation and aggression, making behaviour management in large classes quite difficult. Gladwell refers to the work of Dr Dorothy Lewis, a psychiatrist at New York's Bellevue Hospital and Jonathan Pincus, professor of neurobiology, Yale University which suggests that some aggressive children have a genetic predisposition to lower serotonin and heightened dopamine levels in the brain. When environmental factors are also adverse, these children are prone to aggression. Clearly, the nature and level of support required by a small number of children who remain antisocial, who have severe, pervasive and chronic conditions, may not be able to remain in mainstream schools.

Decisions about special education settings should be made very carefully and within a case management model, where every effort has been made to include children in regular schools, wherever possible. Special education settings provide specialist attention, individual learning and behaviour management plans, and can successfully return many children who are not 'too damaged' to mainstream schools when intervention is early enough, multifaceted and targeted to the child. Successful special education settings share the following characteristics (Kauffman et al, 1995):

- systematic, data-based interventions
- continuous assessment and monitoring of progress
- treatment matched to the child's challenges
- multi-component treatment – academic, social skills, emotional management, therapy
- frequent guided practice of academic and social skills
- programming for transfer and maintenance of skills
- sustained intervention.

Section 4

The Tools of Culture Change

The Tools of Culture Change

Violence response plan

Mediation

Mentoring

Therapeutic games

Crisis interview

Emotional first-aid

TOOLS OF CULTURE CHANGE

The story ends... or does it?

Well, that's almost the end of the story. By the third year we had won a national anti-violence award for reducing violence in our school. What an achievement! I left the Bay to work in Sydney seven years after arriving there. It was heart wrenching to leave – we were all working together so well – all our hard work had paid off and things were pretty peaceful around the school. There was hardly any teasing or harassment, fights in the playground were rare and casual teachers loved working with us! I was transferred to an inner city school where there was lots of work to do and another wonderful headteacher and staff who were working on many of the ideas I had left behind. I negotiated to work on teasing and harassment (my old favourites) and set about teaching small groups of children socio-emotional skills – and yes, mainly at lunch-time. Once again we are well on the way to substantially eliminating violence and harassment in the school.

I returned to the Bay recently – our wonderful deputy was retiring. What a reunion! And what a wonderful witness to the respectful way this woman had worked with children over the years. We had videos of her in there with the kids, reminiscences of her years of service and not a dry eye in the room. I asked about the playground. Everyone said that there was still very little violence – the main source was new kids to the school and those few who needed individual monitoring. However, teasing was on the rise – no one had picked up the work I had been focusing on – interviewing teasers and making targets resilient. The positive playground programmes were still in place, the monitoring systems and immediate responses were still there – it was just my 'little bit' that was missing. I guess there is a lesson in there about making sure support structures are in place to support successful programmes, in spite of personnel coming or going. Must write them a letter…

In Section 4 I have collected many of my favourite 'tools' for culture change. We didn't all use everything all of the time, and some of them I learnt about after leaving the Bay, but I recommend them for your consideration.

One final thought. I've been thinking about the title of my book – Planting the Peace Virus – and the connotations of the word 'virus'. With all the ill effect of viruses that plague the planet at the moment, I've been wondering about why I chose it instead of 'Forest' for example – Planting the Peace Forest. When I look at my mind-maps, I can see that I have used the images of a forest or garden – calm, peaceful. I think the aspect of a virus that attracted me was the active (dare I say aggressive?) nature of a virus. I believe we have to take an active approach to the issues of violence and harassment. I guess throughout my book, I have been trying to create the atmosphere of a calm, peaceful forest with the activity and tenacity of a virus – spreading peace along the way…

ENJOY THE JOURNEY…

11

Violence Response Plan

Following is an example of a violence response plan. The whole school community should have a voice in developing these plans. They will evolve as the school grows and changes. One of the most important points for is as educators is to acknowledge the certainty of change. Once accepted, it becomes easier to adapt and continue the process of learning. The main features of a violence response plan are proactive or preventative strategies that are school-wide, immediate responses to violence and referral to programmes that specifically teach socio-emotional skills to children at risk – along with a big dose of ongoing professional development.

Aims and objectives: To create a systematic, holistic approach to issues of violence, harassment and teasing in a primary school setting. To create an ethos of non-violence.

Proactive Strategies

Activity	Outcomes	Timeframe
Whole-school discussion about non-violence, aggression, rough play	Whole-school commitment to non-violence Working definitions of violence, aggression, rough play, hierarchy of inappropriate behaviour and responses	

Continued…

Activity	Outcomes	Timeframe
Discussion about adults as models of respectful interactions, mindfulness and reflection, language, attitudes	Adults will use respectful language and strategies when dealing with children	
Creation of playground team	Time – frequency, length of meetings Space – where Resources – budget, administration time-in-lieu for team leader, programmes	
Discussion about future schooling, new paradigms, strong teacher-student relationships	New ways of working with children in the classroom	
Socio-emotional development programmes	Social and emotional development becomes part of the mainstream curriculum	
Development of a range of positive playground programmes, eg. raffle, events, student consultation, rule of the week	Fun for children, reinforcement of positive playtime behaviour	
Peer leadership programmes, eg. peer mediation, peer referees, student council	Personal development of student leaders, peer modelling	

Continued...

Activity	Outcomes	Timeframe
Home-school collaboration, eg. parent resource centre, positive communication, information sessions, solution -focused	Positive, friendly, co-operative relationships with parents or carers and community	
Monitoring the playground, data collection and analysis, playground bag, feedback	Current information about playground issues to guide response and focus of resources	

Immediate Response to Violence

- Ensure the safety of all students.
- Immediate withdrawal from the playground for children involved to a prearranged, supervised space, for example, the attention room.
- Application of emotional first-aid (Cool Off, Time-Out) as required.
- Life Space Interview with trained teacher.
- Referral to targeted, remedial programme.

Reactive Strategies

- What – social skills, conflict resolution, teasing and harassment, coping skills, anger management, self-monitoring.
- When – lunch-time works best.
- Where – designated space – 'attention room' (Chill-out Zone).
- Staff – respectful, emotionally intelligent – skilled in mediation, Life Space Interview, mediated learning.
- Parental involvement and referral to outside agencies when problems persist.

Professional Development

What	Who
The school's violence response plan	Whole staff, parents, carers
Long-term nature of violence intervention	Whole staff, parents, carers
Early intervention	Whole staff, parents, carers
Ongoing nature of professional	Whole staff development
Action research	Whole staff
Teaching socio-emotional skills	Whole staff, parents, carers
Emotional intelligence	Whole staff, parents, carers, students
Mindfulness and reflection	Whole staff
Conflict resolution	Whole staff, parents, students
Emotional first-aid	Whole staff, parents, carers, students
Emotional coaching	Volunteers, parents, carers
Mediated learning	Whole staff, parents, carers
Emotional resilience	Whole staff, parents, carers
Circle Time	Whole staff
Mentoring	Volunteers
Therapeutic game leaders	Volunteer teachers, peer leaders
The playground programme	Whole staff, parents, carers, students
Peer leadership	Volunteer teachers, peer leaders
Solution-focused approaches	Whole staff, senior staff
Life Space Interviews	Whole staff, nominated teachers

12

Mediation

I've included this brief outline of the mediation process mainly to show teachers and parents how simple the process can be, especially when mediating for children. I spent many a lunch-time mediating for groups of children on issues that were too complex for our peer mediators – it worked really well with my teenage children as well. The skills are attitudes of a mediator are the most important aspect of the process. Any respectful person who can listen well and referee when things get out of hand can lead others through the steps of mediation to resolve their problems.

Mediation is the process by which a third party helps disputants (people in conflict) work through a set of procedures that will lead them to an agreed solution. Teachers, parents, carers and children can learn to mediate and guide others respectfully through this process. Mediators listen carefully, show empathy and act as referees, ensuring disputants also use respectful ways of communicating during the process. The advantages of training peers to be mediators include the empowerment of students to solve their own conflict, creation of a culture of co-operation in the school, students modelling problem-solving and reduction of teacher involvement with student conflict. Each school should decide which issues peer mediators would work with, depending on the age, skill and experience of the mediators.

The process of mediation includes:

- definition of the problem through questioning of both disputants
- addressing emotions surrounding the problem
- making an analysis of each disputant's needs
- exploring fears and concerns

- creation of options through brainstorming.
- Evaluation of options
- Choosing a solution.

The skills of a mediator include:

Respect: This is demonstrated through the words we use, our body language and our attitudes. Empathy, neutrality and confidentiality are ways of showing respect as mediators.

Reflective listening:
- Use positive body language – eye contact, slightly lean forward, face the person, look interested, nod.
- Ask questions about the problem, feelings about the problems, needs of the disputants, worries of the disputants.
- Say back the main words the speaker is using or the feelings behind the words.

Refereeing: Mediators need to be confident to 'call fouls', like a sports referee, for example, set rules like: take turns talking, no-name calling or put-downs, no shouting. Referees need to know when to call off a mediation session and refer the disputants to a teacher or adjudicator, (for example, headteacher).

Problem-solving: mediators use the steps of problem-solving to guide disputants towards a mutually agreed solution. Problem-solving steps include:

- Brainstorm or make a list of as many options as possible. Suggestions are not evaluated at this point, just accepted and written down. Mediators can make suggestions but must not dominate this important step.
- Evaluate each option by asking, 'Is this a fair option?', 'Does it meet the needs of both people?' and, 'Is this option possible?'
- Choose options with which both disputants agree
- Make a plan for implementing the chosen option(s).

Following is a sample of the steps taken during a mediation session. This format can be used by peers, teachers, parents and carers.

Mediation Steps

Step 1 – Mediator opens session

"Hello, my name is.......................... Welcome to (peer) mediation."

"I would like to remind you of the rules:"

- I will not take sides.
- Each person takes turns talking without interrupting.
- No put-downs or name calling.
- Everything said is confidential.
- Do your best to reach an agreement that is fair.

"Do you both agree?"

Step 2 – Mediator asks questions of both disputants

"What is the problem?"

"How do you feel?"

"What do you need?"

"What are you afraid of or worried about?"

Step 3 – Make a plan

- "Let's brainstorm all possible ideas for a solution. Think of all the ideas that might solve this problem without saying if it is a good idea or not."
- "Now we will look at each idea – evaluate each idea."

  "Is this a fair idea?"

  "Can this idea be done?"

  "Does this idea meet everyone's needs?"
- Decide on one or more solutions.
- Shake hands.

13

Mentoring

While we didn't specifically say 'we are setting up a mentoring programme in our school', in effect, many of us were mentors for children on an informal basis. I have since come across several very successful programmes in my new district. In one programme, volunteers from the community are trained to work with children and come to the school for one hour once a week. They meet with the child for half an hour and then meet with the school co-ordinator for a further 30 minutes to debrief and plan for the next week. They meet in a group and become very supportive of each other as well as their 'mentees'. There has been a plethora of volunteers – more than can be given mentees.

Mentors help others grow and develop by getting to know them in semi-structured meetings. Relationships are built by focusing together on a task, for example, academic skills, socio-emotional skills, personal development, and sport. Among the benefits of mentoring are improvements in behaviour and attendance and changes in teacher attitude to mentees (child receiving help). Mentors can help children with reading, maths, spelling, sports skills, anger management, friendship skills, resilience, transitions, confidence, optimism and work habits. Mentors can be teachers, parents, carers, grandparents, community volunteers, older peers, local businesses and childhood education students. The mentor usually visits the student for about half an hour per week for up to one school year.

Mentor qualities	Mentor skills
Emotional intelligence	Empathy – eye contact
Persistence	Reflective listening
Dependability	Positive self-talk
Respect	Strengths-based approaches
Commitment	Solution focusing
Optimism	
Interest	

Strategies for Mentors

- Help children identify realistic goals, skills and needs – academic, behavioural, emotional.
- Explain, teach and demonstrate skills.
- Encourage persistence – express confidence and optimism.
- Encourage a love of learning – participating in lessons.
- Help children with friendship skills, playing games.
- Provide feedback to teachers and parents or carers.
- Celebrate successes – keep track of progress.

Mentor training: Basic training for mentors should include the following topics:

- communicating with children
- importance of boundaries
- confidentiality
- child protection and limited confidentiality
- encouragement, specific praise, strengths-based approaches
- social skills training
- anti-bullying strategies
- planning and setting goals – solution-focused.

Procedures

- Co-ordinator trains mentors, matches mentors with mentees, debriefs mentors, checks for over involvement, discusses procedures.

- Semi-structured meeting once per week for half an hour, either first or last thing in the day – stuffed toy or puppet used for connection with the mentee – box of resources, for example, academic programme, social skills activities, games, including playground games.
- Debriefing session for half an hour after meeting mentees-gives feedback, encourages mentors to bond as a group, looks at positives, negatives, things of interest, what to do differently.

14

The Life Space Interview

This is one of my favourite strategies when working with children in emotional crisis. Once you have identified the values and motives behind the child's actions, you can join with them in the problem-solving phase – works like magic. Sometimes you have to keep up the emotional first-aid for quite a while, but if the student has had anger management lessons or has an emotional coach, then they will already know what their most effective calming responses will be.

The following scenario serves to demonstrate the steps of a life space interview. While there is a basic pattern to the interview, one moves back and forth between the steps as the interview progresses. In this example, a teacher is dealing with one of two boys involved in a fight.

Pre-interview: Apply emotional first-aid. Allow children time to gain emotional control by suggesting physical strategies like having a drink of water, taking some deep breaths, splashing one's face with water, walking to another venue together. Some children need a lot of space at this time. Once the child is beginning to talk, they are ready to engage in the interview.

Comment: The object of emotional first-aid is to reduce the emotional intensity of the child's reactions before engaging in a formal interview. It may be necessary to repeat this step if a child loses emotional control during the formal interview.

Step 1.   Establish an empathic connection

Teacher: Take a seat, John. You have had a chance to calm down now, so I hope you are feeling better. Do you feel like you could talk about what happened?

John: (mumbles) I don't know

Teacher: Well let's have a go. If you start feeling angry again or
            need a break, let me know. The playground teacher told
            me you were hitting Tim at lunch-time. You must have
            been feeling pretty upset to hit him. How come you
            decided to hit Tim?

John: He called me an idiot. He always calls me an idiot.

Teacher: That would have made you feel pretty mad. It's not a
            nice name and you are certainly not an idiot.

John: He always calls me an idiot.

Teacher: So this has been happening for some time now. I wish I
            had known, maybe we could have worked out something
            better than all this name-calling and fighting.

John: (mumbles) Hhmm.

Teacher: I guess I wouldn't like it either if I was being called
            names all the time.

Comment: During step 1, support and understanding of the child's
distress is conveyed through reflective listening, empathic statements,
pacing and time. Be mindful of your own emotions, reactions and
attitudes to the situation, acknowledge them and let them go. Use
language that reflects respect, control, assistance. This step ends
when the child starts to use words to communicate.

**Step 2.   Encourage the child to talk by focusing on
            the incident**

Teacher: What was happening when he called you that name?

John: We were playing tips and he kept getting me in.

Teacher:	And you got frustrated when he kept getting you in?
John:	He can run faster than I can and he always catches me. He keeps on getting me in and he got everyone else to pick on me too. He's so stupid!
Teacher:	John, we don't use put-downs. You know how bad you feel when it happens to you, don't you? I can see how you would have felt angry and frustrated though. Who else was playing with you and Tim?
John:	Joseph, Hassan and Josh and some other kids, not sure who else.
Teacher:	Were they being caught too?
John:	Not much. They're Tim's friends so they do what ever he says.
Teacher:	When did you first start to feel angry?
John:	They all started laughing at me when I said it wasn't fair. I just got so mad.
Teacher:	So, you were playing with Tim and his mates and you noticed you were getting caught a lot and said it wasn't fair. Then they laughed and you started to feel angry. Some pushing and shoving turned into a fight and the teacher came.
John:	Yeah.

Comment: During step 2, the teacher asks questions to gain an understanding of the child's perception of the incident. This step ends when talk has produced a review of time, place and people involved and the emotional intensity is lowered.

Step 3   Values, central issues and therapeutic goals

Teacher: It sounds like playing fair is important to you – sounds like you think people should be polite to each other while playing, is that right?

John: I don't know. I guess so

Teacher: These are good values and very important. But I think things fell apart when you chose hitting as a way to solve the problem. What do you think?

John: I didn't decide to hit him, I was just feeling mad and everyone was laughing. I just hit him.

Teacher: Oh, so anger came along and stopped you thinking of better ways to solve this problem. That happens. What's your body's first sign that you are getting angry? Remember the other day when we were talking about emotional first-aid in class?

John   Oh...yeah, I remember...um, mine was tight fists, yeah, they were tight.

Teacher: Hitting Tim got you into trouble with our rules at school. What do you know about our 'Hands Off' rule?

John: Don't hit anyone.

Teacher: Do you agree that this is a fair rule?

John: I don't know, sort of.

Teacher: When children hurt each other to solve their problems, the teachers, mums and dads think it is a serious problem and we work together to find other solutions. We all feel mad or frustrated sometimes and we need ways to handle our feelings that don't hurt anyone.

There are lots of things people can do to be in charge of their anger. I know we have learnt a bit about it in class, but I think you might need a few more skills and a bit more practice. I think it will help you to go to the chill out zone at lunch-time to learn more about anger management.

John: (nods)

Teacher: It seems like there are some difficulties between you and Tim that have to be sorted out. Tim might need help to stop name-calling too.

John: (nods)

Teacher: Maybe our peer mediators will be able to help.

Comment: During step 3, the child's feelings, values and motives are explored through their account of the incident and central issues are identified. This step ends when the issue has been stated concisely and therapeutic goals are chosen. In this scenario, the teacher identifies anger management, name-calling and ongoing tension as the central issues and anger management as the therapeutic goal.

Step 4   Problem-solving, consequences and restitution

Teacher: So thinking back to when you first felt angry, what might have been a better way to handle what was happening in the game – something that wouldn't get you into trouble for hurting others?

John: I don't know. Nothing. Maybe I should have walked away.

Teacher: Did you think of doing that at the time?

John: No, I guess I was too mad already.

Teacher: Walking away is a good way to calm down. It gives you time to think of what to do. Walk away, have a drink of water and tell yourself not to worry about it. What could you have done instead of hitting Tim when he called you a name?

John: Maybe I could have said stop calling me names but he wouldn't stop, I know he wouldn't.

Teacher: If he didn't stop when you asked, what could you have done then?

John: Play somewhere else or tell a teacher

Teacher: Getting help from a teacher is a good idea when others don't stop. So, we've been able to think of a few choices other than hitting next time there is a name-calling problem. Maybe we have to talk with all the kids in your class about playing fairly. Maybe we could change the rules of that game to make it fairer. I'll talk to your teacher about it. What do you think?

John: It might work – I don't know, I think Tim just doesn't like me.

Teacher: Mmm, maybe he doesn't but we still have to be polite at school, and hopefully friendly with each other. What do you think you can do to fix the problem now?

John: Keep away from Tim I guess and maybe play with someone else.

Teacher: Sounds OK. What about the idea of you and Tim seeing the peer mediators? What do you think of that idea?

John: I don't know, I don't think it will help, he just always picks on me.

Teacher:	Well, there is a problem between you and Tim and either you have to work it out together or with mediators or the headteacher and your parents. How about you try with the peer mediators, and if that doesn't help, I'll be mediator between you and Tim, what do you think?
John:	OK.
Teacher:	You know, there were quite a few little kids standing around watching you and Tim. It might have been a bit scary for them, or the teacher. What might you do to fix this?
John:	Say sorry to the teacher and not fight in the playground.
Teacher:	I think these are great ideas. So, it sounds like the plan is that you and Tim both visit the chill out zone tomorrow during lunch-time for mediation and anger management training. I'll talk to your teacher about the rules for the game and see if we can make it fairer. I'll ring your parents and let them know about what has happened and what you have decided to do. I'll write out this plan and see how it is going tomorrow.

Comment: During step 4, problem-solving strategies are used to create a range of alternative solutions. The teacher identifies a need for staff to investigate the game and help children to play fairly. Consequences are applied in a matter-of-fact manner. This step ends when the child is able to put solutions into words

Step 5   Planning for success

Teacher:	How do you think things will go with Tim between now and tomorrow?
John:	I'll just stay away from him.

Teacher:	That should work out OK. What if he says something rude to you?
John:	I'll just walk away and get help from a teacher or you.
Teacher:	That's probably a good idea, especially if you haven't been to the peer mediators yet. I'm going to see Tim after we finish talking, so I'll be asking him the same sorts of questions – asking him to make a plan about getting along with others at school. Is there anything that is worrying you? Anything else you might need to be successful with this plan?
John:	Maybe John's friends will try to get me into trouble.
Teacher:	What might you do if that happens?
John:	Get help from a teacher.
Teacher:	Now you're thinking! Of course I will help you if that happens. What might you do if you start feeling angry again?
John:	I'll go to the chill out zone and learn some more about being angry.
Teacher:	Excellent idea. The headteacher will want to know about your plans for fixing this problem. She thinks children can usually manage their own problems but she has to make sure school is safe for everyone. I'll let her know about your plans, but if things don't turn out after you try mediation and apologising, then the head will have to talk with you and your parents about what else could be done to help you. But I don't think it will get to that, do you?
John:	No, I guess not.

Teacher: Anyway, good luck with your plan, I think it should work. I'll check with you tomorrow to see how you are going with it.

Comment: During step 5, the child rehearses what will happen and anticipates, with the teacher, the range of reactions possible from others. This step ends when talks about how they will handle the current issue and plans for dealing with future similar events.

Step 6   Re-entering normal activities

Teacher: It's time to go back to class soon. What is your class doing now?

John: We are in the library after lunch.

Teacher: Well, how do you feel about going back to class?

John: OK I guess.

Teacher: Is there anything else you would like to talk about right now? Are you worried about anything else at school?

John: Not really.

Teacher: Who would you talk to if you needed help at school?

John: Well, you and Ms Barlow, last year's teacher. She was nice.

Teacher: That's great. Let's take a walk over to the library to see if they are there. What do you like best about the library?

Comment: During step 6, the child is prepared for closure of the interview and re-entry into the peer group. This step ends when the child seems ready to re-enter the group in a responsible way.

15

Emotional First-aid

The notion of emotional first-aid follows on from the idea that our emotions are a mixture of cognitive and physiological processes. Children were amazingly open to these ideas, especially when I drew pictures of their brains and how our thoughts can start a physical reaction that floods our bodies with neuropeptides. This in no way 'excuses' anyone from over-reacting while angry and hurting others. When we understand the process, we are able to intervene early – in response to our body's early warning signs – and use a range of self-calming strategies. Emotional first-aid works best when someone – a mentor, parent, teacher, emotional coach – spends time explaining emotional reactions to children and helping them identify and practise their preferred anger management strategy. Then, in a time of crisis, it is easier for the child to self-monitor and calm themselves down.

Emotional first-aid recognises the physiological nature of anger and aims to create time and space for the body's response to calm down. Teachers, parents, carers, emotional coaches, mentors and peer referees can use simple strategies to help children gain control of their emotions. Once children can recognise their own body's early warning signs, they can monitor themselves and learn self-regulation by applying the calming strategies that work best for them.

First Step – Early Warning Signs

At a calm time, before an emotional crisis occurs, discuss anger management with the child and help them determine where they experience their body's first signs of anger. If children do not know where their body feels anger, invite them to close their eyes and relax while you describe a scene that might cause anger. Ask them to imagine that they are having been waiting for a long time and someone pushes in front of them in the line. When they open their eyes, they are most likely able to say where they first feel anger. Talk about where you feel anger. Mention places where people might feel anger, for example, fists, neck, chest, head, knees or shoulders. Most people can identify where they feel anger. Let them know that this is good, because it is the body's way of letting you know so then you can do something about it.

Second Step – Fuse Length

Identify how long their 'fuse' is. That is, how long between when they first feel anger (in their fist, chest, head, shoulders etc.) and when they are no longer able to think straight. Some children have fuses that are a matter of seconds long, for others they might have up to ten seconds before they 'lose it'. Using a stopwatch adds an element of fun and understanding. Working out the 'fuse length' helps children see the importance of using emotional first-aid quickly, before they stop thinking straight.

Third Step – Self-calming

Work with the child to choose a range of strategies to try the next time anger comes along. Following are physical and cognitive (thinking) strategies that children might try to calm themselves:

Physical Responses

- Have a drink of water. Water helps cool the child and reduce the biomolecular response while the time taken and physical exertion required to obtain water also helps reduce physiological responses.
- Breath control. Controlled, even breathing helps maintain the oxygen – carbon dioxide bio-feedback balance and reduce feelings of panic. Count the breaths '1 2 3 in – 1 2 3 out' – or any number of equal counts, depending on the natural rate of breath. Counting breaths also has a meditative effect.
- Take a walk. Walking helps reduce physiological responses and allows time to pass. Have children count their breath in time with their steps.

- Ask for space. Some children need to be left alone for a while to calm themselves. Move away and allow the child some time unbothered.

Cognitive scripts (Positive self-talk)

- Calming self-talk can help children settle. Use scripts such as 'Don't worry about it', 'Take it easy', 'Calm down', 'Have a drink of water.'
- Confident self-talk can remind children that they can solve problems, for example, 'You can work this out', 'It will be OK', 'You've worked this out before', 'You can do it.'

When an Emotional Crisis Occurs

When a child is having an emotional outburst, many of the following physical and cognitive signs will be observable:

Physical symptoms	Cognitive symptoms
red, sweaty face	shouting
short breath	swearing
wide eyes, frowning looks	angry words
agitated and aggressive actions	irrational thinking

Quietly suggest they choose and try one of their 'pre-determined' strategies. Be prepared for the physiological response to take up to twenty minutes to reduce. Wait until the child has regained composure before entering into a life space interview. Reflective listening is a good strategy to help calm agitated thoughts and words. Reflective listening is a simple strategy that conveys empathy and understanding using the following strategies:

- Say back the content of what the child says, for example, 'You were playing a game when he called you a loser'.
- Say what you think the child is feeling based on what has been said and on body language, for example, 'It sounds like you were getting frustrated with the situation'.
- Show that you understand the child's point of view and values.

16

Therapeutic Games

Kids love therapeutic games. Kids love any games but therapeutic games takes advantage of their love of play to teach them socio-emotional skills. This is such an easy way to get their attention – and even when I ran them at lunch-time, the kids begged to play them again and again. Once I realised how effective a tool they were, I began to design more and more of them – last count is nine games and I still have more I want to create. (See Further Resources p163)

Therapeutic games are designed to teach social and emotional skills to groups of children in a fun way. Besides being an excellent way to build rapport, playing the games allows discussion of social and emotional problems to emerge in naturalistic ways. Playing the games with a skilled game leader provides a safe and supportive environment in which children learn and practise new skills. While playing the games, problems sometimes arise giving leaders the opportunity to help children resolve the problem in friendly ways.

Promoting emotional resilience through therapeutic games

Prosocial skills are the 'social oil' that makes getting on together that much easier. Social competence, emotional resilience and problem-solving skills are critical in a changing world that will rely increasingly on collaborative approaches to learning and dealing with problems in future workplaces. Early intervention is vital for children who have difficulty getting along with others. Through direct instruction, modelling of social skills, guided practice and meaningful opportunities to try new skills, children learn the basics needed to relate positively with others.

Emotional resilience is the ability to bounce back after a crisis and is an important factor in the lives of children dealing with disadvantage in their lives. When children have a network of supportive adults and a repertoire of adaptive personal skills to call upon, they can cope, even when there are large gaps in some areas of their lives. Playing therapeutic games with a skilled leader can help vulnerable children develop emotional resilience.

Game leaders

Game leaders can be psychologists, counsellors, specialist teachers, teachers, parents, carers, grandparents, mentors, peer mediators, peer support leaders, scripture teachers, in fact, whoever is prepared to respectfully referee children and work through the issues that come up while playing the games. During the game, leaders teach the basic teaching points, apply emotional first-aid, if needed, and conduct brief Life Space Interviews as required. Game leaders need the following skills:

Mediated learning: Play is the language of children and important to their development. As they play they learn skills that will help them meet the physical, social, thinking and language challenges of their lives. When adults 'mediate' between the child and their social environment, in the case of therapeutic games, they increase the chances of them acquiring social skills like taking turns, explaining, negotiating, fitting in with others, sharing, and emotional control skills like anger management and coping. Leaders can increase children's skills by modelling, adding meaning and context to the skills and using 'scripts' to provide the words and ideas needed to resolve social problems, making it more likely that the child will transfer the skills to future situations.

Modelling prosocial skills: Game leaders look for opportunities to model prosocial skills, for example, using manners, taking turns, saying sorry and resolving conflicts in friendly ways. Mimes, scripts and little role-plays are used to show children what assertiveness looks like, what positive self-talk sounds like, how to seek help or what words mean. Leaders also look for and refer to peers who are using prosocial skills during the game. Smiling, having fun and being respectful are also modelled.

Importance of language: Language is central to the human experience, allowing communication with self and others, and guiding our construction of reality. There is reciprocity between the words we use and the attitudes we hold. While playing the games, leaders carefully choose language that reflects respect, calmness and confidence. Non-judgmental language encourages children to take responsibility for their actions and develop empathy for others. Following are samples of scripts to use while playing. Further script samples are provided with each game.

- Oh well, not every one can go first – I'll be first some other time.
- It's hard but I can wait for my turn.
- Don't worry about it, calm down, it's not worth getting upset about.
- What could we try to solve this problem?

Verbal reinforcers: Specific positive comments made to children during the game are a powerful way to reinforce prosocial skills and build positive self-concepts. Verbal reinforcers need to be specific, immediate and applied liberally to be effective, for example:

- I like the way you kept trying to work out solutions
- It's great that you waited for your turn even though it was hard.
- That was good listening (waiting, sharing, helping, encouraging, comforting, etc.)
- Thank you for sharing (waiting listening, being kind, etc.)
- That was a fair (kind, friendly, etc.) thing to do.
- I can see being fair (honest, helpful, etc.) is important to you.

Immediacy: Leaders constantly look for 'teachable moments'. When a child uses a prosocial skill that the leader wishes to reinforce in others, a verbal reinforcement is given immediately. When a player lands on a teaching point in the game, the leader draws attention to it through discussion. Likewise, when interpersonal conflict arises, the leader halts the game and leads the disputants through the emotional control (as needed) and problem-solving processes. Leaders may orchestrate 'mini crises' to create teachable moments, for example, by asking who wants to go first. Almost every child will want to, creating conflict between players. This creates the opportunity to lead a discussion about fair ways of deciding who goes first. Children will have a myriad of ideas which would have been lost if the leader simply chose the first player. Leaders may call upon children who did not care if they went first or not to explain why it didn't matter, thus providing peer models of alternative responses. It also allows the leader to make scripted comments like 'it doesn't matter if you don't go first', 'everyone gets a turn', 'I'll just wait for my turn', etc. Stacking the cards is another way of directing the play – but don't get caught!

Discipline: Negotiate rules such as turn taking, talking quietly and listening to each other at the beginning of the game. Most are eager to play and will co-operate and encourage others to keep the rules. Model the rules, for example, waiting silently and patiently for children to listen after having asked them to listen. Suggesting that they will have to come back in the next break will motivate those who do not like giving up lunch breaks to solve problems. Use emotional coaching to help children work through crises. If a child cheats, ask the group if they would all like to play with the same rules as the cheater. The rules can be flexible, but only if everyone agrees.

If the group is too unruly, stop the game saying, in a matter of fact manner, 'Let's try again next week'. Let the children know you would really like to play the game with them. Ask them what sorts of things would help make it easier to play the game next week. Reduce the group size and include a child with strong prosocial skills. This prosocial child's position could be rotated among the other children in the class who are keen to be included in a game.

Curious stance: An attitude of curiosity helps when dealing with crises. Being neutral, respectful, supportive and un-emotive will help establish a stress free environment in which children can try out their new skills.

Awareness of reading skills: In order to avoid embarrassment, leaders need to help poor readers without drawing attention to their difficulties. Some concepts will need explanation and discussion to ensure understanding. It is good practice for the game leader to read out the hints, strategies and concepts discovered during the game. Curiously, many children, even those with reading difficulties, will insist on reading their own cards and do quite well at it.

Incentives: Every child player wins a prize. Children enjoy receiving something as simple as a sticker or an award or a lucky dip at the end of the game. This adds to the fun and motivation and ameliorates the pain of not finishing first in the game. Avoid making 'winning' a big issue by talking about finishing the game, not winning the game. Every player 'wins'.

17

Commercial Resources

Lucky Duck is the UK's largest publisher of the type of resources mentioned. They have books and videos on:

ADHD
Anger Management
Asperger's Syndrome and Autism
Behaviour Management
Bullying
Circle Time
Citizenship and PSHE
Eating Disorders
Emotional Literacy
Peer Support
Self-esteem
Social Skills
Stress Management

Visit **www.luckyduck.co.uk**

Two major suppliers of a variety of publishers who carry similar titles are:

Incentive Plus: **www.incentiveplus.co.uk**
Smallwood Publishing Ltd: **www.smallwood.co.uk**

References

Bandura, A. (1986) *Social Foundations of Thought and Action: A Social Cognitive Theory*, Englewood Cliffs, NJ: Prentice-Hall

Beare, H. (2001) *Creating the future school: Student outcomes and the reform of education*, London: Routledge Falmer.

Begley, P. T. & Johansson, O. (eds) (2003) *The ethical dimensions of school leadership*, Dordtrecht, Netherlands: Kruwer Academic Press.

Benard, B. (1997) *Fostering Resilience in Children, Champaign*, Ill.: ERIC Clearinghouse on Elementary and Early Childhood Education.

Berger, E. H. (2000) *Parents as partners in education: The school and home working together*, New York: Merrill

Behrman, R. E. (ed) (1995) *'The Future of Children', Special issue: Long-term outcomes of early childhood programmes*, 5(3). Available form: The David and Lucile Packard Foundation, Center for the Future of Children, Los Altos, CA

Blum, R. (2000) *Healthy Youth development: A Resiliency Paradigm for Adolescent Health Development*, 3rd pacific Rim Conference of the International Association for Adolescent Health: Lincoln University, Christchurch, June.

Butler, K. (1997) The anatomy of resilience. *Family Therapy Networks*, March/April, 22-31.

Christenson, S.L., Rounds, T. & Franklin, M. J. (1992) 'Home-school collaboration: Effects, issues and opportunities'. In S.L. Christenson and J.C. Conoley (eds) Home-school collaboration: *Enhancing children's academic and social competence*, pp 19-51. Silver Spring, MD: National Association of School Psychologists.

Clark, R.M. (1983) *Family life and school achievement*, Chicago: University of Chicago Press.

DeChillo, N., Koren, P. E. & Mezera, M. (1996) 'Families and Professionals in Partnership'. In B. A. Stroul (ed) *Childrens' Mental Health: Creating systems of care in a changing society*, pp 389-407. Baltimore: Brookes.

De Shazer, S. (1994) *Words were originally magic*, New York: W. W. Norton.

Donnellan, A. M. & LaVigna, G. W., Negri-Shoultz, N. & Fassbender, L. L. (1988) *Progress without Punishment: Effective approaches for learners with behaviour problems*, Teachers College Press: Teachers College, Columbia University, New York and London.

Durant, M. (1995) *Creative strategies for school problems*, New York: W. W. Norton.

Edgar, D. (1999) 'Families as the crucible of competence in a changing social ecology'. In E. Frydenberg (ed) Learning to Cope: *Developing as a Person in Complex Societies*, pp 109-129. Oxford University Press, Oxford

Edgar, D. (2003) *'Windows of Opportunity: The changing context of early childhood development'*. (Paper prepared for Building Blocks for Life and Learning: A public Education Council forum on early childhood education, Sydney, Australia, July 9th, 2003).

Embry, D. E., Flannery, D., Vazsony, A., Powell, K. & Atha, H. (1996) 'Peace Builders: A theoretically driven, school-based model for early violence prevention'. *American Journal of Preventative Medicine*, Vol 22, pp 91-100.

Families First NSAW Plan – Support network for families raising children. http://www.parenting.nsw.gov.au/public/s26_homepage/

Feuerstein, R. (1980) *Instrumental Enrichment*, Baltimore, MD.: University Park Press

Fuller, A. (1998) *From surviving to thriving: Promoting mental health in young people*, ACER Press, Victoria, Australia

Fuller, A. (2001) http://www.projectresilience.com

Gardner, H. (1999) *Intelligence Reformed: Multiple intelligences for the 21st Century*, New York, NY: Basic Books

Giroux, H. (1985) 'Intellectual Labour and Pedagogical Work: re-thinking the role of the teacher as intellectual', *Phenomenology and Pedagogy*, 5 (1), pp 20-32

Gladwell, M. (1997) 'Damaged: Why do some people turn into violent criminals?', *The New Yorker*, February 24, pp 132-138.

Glasser, W. (1990) *The Quality School: Managing students without Coercion*. Harper and Row, Publishers, London

Goleman, D. (1996) *Emotional Intelligence: Why it can matter more than IQ*, Bloomsbury Publishing, London.

Goleman, D. (2000) 'Leadership that gets results', *Harvard Business Review*, March, pp 78-90.

Gottman, J.M., Fainsilber Katz, L. & Hooven, C. (1997) *Meta-Emotion: How Families Communicate Emotionally*, Laurence Erlbaun Associates, Publishers, New Jersey

Greenwood, P.W., Model, K., Rydell, P. & Chiesa, J. 1996) *Diverting children from a life of Crime: Measuring Cost and Benefits*. RAND Corporation: United States

Grose, M., (2004) Young Leaders Program: A leadership programmes for students from Year 5 to Year 8, http://www.parentingideas.com.au

Haim, G. (1972) *Managing behaviour without coercion*, New York: Macmillan

Hallet, C. & Birchall, E. (1992) *Co-ordination and child protection: a review of the literature*, Edinburgh: HMSO.

Hawley, D. R. & DeHaan, L. (1996) Toward a definition of family resilience: Integrating life-span and family perspectives. *Family Processes*, 35(3), 283-298.

Hitchcock, G., Hughes, D. (1995) *Research and the teacher*, London, New York: Routledge

Holly, M. (1989) 'Reflective Writing and the Spirit of Inquiry', *Cambridge Journal of Education*. Vol 19 (1).

Ireland National Children's Plan. http://www.nco.ie

Johnson, N. (2001) 'Leading and managing innovation and improvement', *School Leadership Preparation Programme*. NSW Department of Education and Training, Australia.

Johnson, D. W. & Johnson, R. T. (1996) 'Conflict resolution and Peer mediation in elementary and secondary schools: A review of the research', *Review of Educational Research*, Vol 66 (4) pp 459-506.

Jordan, J. (1997) 'A Narrative Account of a Teacher Researching and Changing Her Classroom Practice', *Teaching and Teachers' Work*. Vol 5 (2), pp 1-9.

(Available form the School of Education, The Flinders University of South Australia).

Karoly, L. A., Greenwood, P. W., Everingham, S. S., Hoube, J., Kilburn, M. R., Rydell, C. P. & Chiesa, J. (1998) *Investing in our children: what we know and don't know about the costs and benefits of early childhood interventions*, Santa Monica, CA: RAND

Kazdin, A. (1987) *Conduct disorders in childhood and adolescence*, London: Sage.

Kauffman, J. M., Lloyd, J. W., Baker, J. & Riedel, T. M. (1995) 'Inclusion of all students with emotional or behavioural disorders? Lets think again', *Phi Delta Kappan*, March, pp 542-546.

Kozulin, A., Gindis, B., Ageyev, V. S. & Miller, S. M. (2003) *Vygotsky's educational theory in cultural context*, Cantry: Cambridge University Press.

Kukic, S. (1995) *'Families and communities together'*, Paper presented at the Utah FACT Initiative Conference, Salt Lake City.

Lantieri, L. & Patti, J. (1996) *Waging Peace in Our Schools*, Boston: Beacon Press

Lewkowicz, A. (1999) *Teaching Emotional Intelligence: making informed choices*, Cheltenham, Vic.: Hawker Brownlow Education

MacMillan, D., Gresham, F.M., & Forness, S. (1991) Full Inclusion: An empirical perspective. *Behaviour Disorders*, 21 (2), 145-159.

Maines, B. & Robinson, G. (1997) *Crying for Help: the No Blame Approach to Bullying*. Bristol, Lucky Duck Publishing

Mapping Sure Start Scotland: http://www.scotland.gov.uk/edru/

Mayer, G. R. & Sulzer-Azaroff, B. (1990) 'Interventions for vandalism'. In G. Stoner, M. R. Shinn, & H. M. Walker (eds) *Interventions for achievement and behaviour problems*, Monograph. Washington DC: National Association of School Psychologists. pp 559-580.

Olweus, D. (1993) *Bullying: What We Know and What We Can Do*. Oxford: Blackwell Publishers

Pert, C. B. (1999) *Molecules of Emotion: The science behind mind-body medicine*, Simon & Schuster: New York.

Perry, B. (1996) *The Mismatch between Opportunity and Investment*, CIVATAS Initiative Chicago.

Pikas, A. (1989) The Common Concern Method for the treatment of Mobbing. In E. Roland, & E. Munthe, *Bullying: An International Perspective*. London, David Fulton

Pogrow, S. (2001) 'Avoiding Comprehensive Schoolwide Reform Models', *Educational Leadership*, May, pp 82-83.

Putnam, R. D. (2002) *Democracies in flux: The Evolution of Social Capital in Contemporary society*. New York: Oxford University Press

Redl, F. (1966) *When We Deal With Children*, The Free Press, New York

Reid, J. (1993). Prevention of conduct disorder before and after school entry: Relating interventions to developmental findings. *Development and Psychopathology*, Vol 5 (1/2) pp 243-262.

Rigby K. (2002) *A Meta-Evaluation of Methods and Approaches to Reducing Bullying in Pre-schools and Early Primary school in Australia*. National Crime

Prevention programme, Canberra: Commonwealth Attorney General's Department

Roerdan, L. P. (2001) 'Reclaiming Children and Youth'. *Journal of Emotional and Behavioural Problems*, Vol 10 (1). pp 24-28.

Saleebey, S. D. (1992) *The Strengths Perspective in Social Work Practice*, New York: Longman.

Salovey, P. & Sluyte, D. (eds) (1997) *Emotional Development and Emotional Intelligence: Educational implications*, New York: Basic Books

Schon, D. (1983) *The Reflective practitioner: How professionals think in action*, USA: Basic Books Inc.

Scott, D. (1993) 'Inter-agency collaboration: Why is it so difficult? Can we do it better?' *Children Australia*, Vol (18) No (4) pp 4-9.

Skuy, M. (1997) *Mediated Learning in and out of the Classroom*, Melbourne: Hawker Brownlow Education.

Smith, B. (1993) *Addressing the Delusion of Relevance: Struggles in connecting educational research and social justice*, (Unpublished paper)

Smyth, J. (1986) *Educational Leadership in Schools: Reflection in Action*, Geelong: Deakin University Press

Smyth, J. (1987) 'Teachers as intellectuals in a critical pedagogy of schooling', *Education and Society*, Vol 5, 1&2, pp 11-28.

Smyth, J. (1992) 'Teachers' Work and the Politics of Reflection', *American Educational Research Journal*, Vol 29 (2), pp 267-300.

Stomfay-Stitz, A. (1994) 'Conflict Resolution and Peer Mediation: Pathways to safer schools', *Childhood Education*, pp 279-282.

Sugai, G. & Horner, R. (1994) 'Including students with severe behaviour problems in general education settings: Assumptions, challenges and solutions'. In J. Mart, G. Sugai, & G. Tindal (eds) *The Oregon Conference monograph*, Vol 6, pp 102-120, Eugene: University of Oregon.

Sugai, G. & Horner, R. (2001) *School Climate and Discipline: going to scale. National Summit on the Shared Implementation of IDEA*, Washington DC.

Sure Start – United Kingdom. http://www.surestart.gov.uk/home.cfm

Tonry, M. & Farrington, D. P. (eds) (1995) *Building a safer society: Strategic approaches to crime prevention*, The University of Chicago Press: Chicago.

Vygotsky, L. S. (1976) 'Play and its role in the mental development of the child'. In J. S. Bruner, A. Jolly, & K. Sylvia (eds) *Play – Its role in development and evolution*, pp 537-554. New York: Basic Books.

Vygotsky, L. S. (1986) *Thought and Language*, Cambridge, Mass: MIT Press

Walker, H. M., Colvin, G. & Ramsey, E. (1995) *Antisocial behaviour in schools: Strategies and best practices*, Pacific grove, CA: Brooks/Cole

Walker, H. M., Horner, R. H., Sugai, G., Bullis, M., Sprague, J. R., Bricker, D. & Kaufman, M. J. (1996) 'Integrated approaches to preventing antisocial behaviour patterns among school aged children', *Journal of Emotional and Behaviour Disorders*, Vol. 4 (4), pp 194-211.

Walsh, F. (1996) The concept of family resilience: Crisis and Challenge. *family Processes*, 35(3) 261-281.

Witt, J. & Marsten, D. (1983) 'Assessing the acceptability of behavioural interventions', *Psychology in the Schools*, Vol 20, pp 510-517.

Witt, J. & Robbins, J. (1985) 'Acceptability of reductive interventions for the control of inappropriate child behaviour', *Journal of Abnormal Psychology*, Vol 11, pp 59-67.

Wood, M. & Long, N. (1991) *Life Space Intervention*, PRO-ED, Austen, Texas

Zigler, E., Taussig, C. & Black, K. (1992) 'Early childhood intervention: A promising preventative for juvenile delinquency', *American Psychologist*, Vol 47 (8), pp 997-1006.

Zimmerman, B. J. (1991) 'A social cognitive view of self-regulated academic learning. *Journal of Educational Psychology*, Vol 81, pp 329-339.

Further Resources

We hope to expand our range of publications to include games. We have avoided these in the past because of the problems of printing and packing boards, cards etc. With improved printing technology available in schools we intend to trial putting all the required resources onto a CD for schools to produce themselves. We have included some of Robyn's ideas about her games, which will be published soon to complement this book.

The Games

Following is a set of therapeutic games created by the Robyn to be used as part of a school's response to violence and harassment. The games are remedial in nature and are generally played at lunch-time with small groups of children identified as needing extra tuition in socio-emotional skills. They can also be played with individual children or larger groups of children as part of classroom programmes. The games are progressive in terms of skill development and complexity and have a strong focus on early intervention (ages range from 4 to 14). The games may be used sequentially over 6 to 8 sessions to cover a range of social and emotional skills, or in one-off sessions to cover specific skills. Socio-emotional development addressed by the games include:

- social skills (Little Friends, Road Race, Friendly Island – Lonely Island)
- friendship skills (Friendly Friends)
- anger management skills (Think Again)
- coping with teasing (Tease)
- coping in the playground (Playground)
- paying compliments (Give Me Strength)

Little Friends, Road Race, Friendly Island – Lonely Island

These three games teach the language and skills of friendships and emotional vocabulary to children aged 4 to 9 years old. Friendly and unfriendly actions are discussed as cards are turned over during the game. While playing together, children practise basic game-playing skills like turn taking, waiting, using manners, talking and listening, co-operation and dealing with not finishing first. These three games have increasingly complex boardfaces that prepare children for the more complex games that follow.

Friendly Friends

'Friendly Friends' is a game about friendships designed for children aged between 4 and 12. Social dilemmas are presented for players to solve. The concepts of friendship, friendliness, politeness and conflict are discussed. It is explained to children that they do not have to be friends with everyone at school but they are expected to be polite, and hopefully friendly. With this understanding, children tend to be more accepting of others and more likely to include them in games. Playing the game with children who exclude or are mean to others can be an effective way to encourage politeness, friendliness and kindness while outlining behaviour expectations.

Think Again

'Think Again' teaches children aged 6 to 14 about managing anger and thinking before they act. Conflicts are read out for players to solve in friendly ways. A range of self-calming ideas are presented like talking sense to oneself, taking time to calm down, having a drink of water and getting help from adults. The game includes consequences for aggressive solutions by tossing the Decision Cube or a coin. The difference between being assertive and being aggressive is explored.

Tease

'Tease' is designed to help targets of teasing aged 7 to 14 develop emotional resilience and must be played with a skilled game leader. Kids who tease can also learn something about empathy by playing the game, but 'bullies' do not usually respond to this strategy. Playing the game provides an opportunity to practise new skills while desensitising children to the experience of teasing. Players are told of their right to attend school without being teased or harassed. They identify adults to approach if help is needed and explore different responses, including things to say and do. An environment is created where players can discuss their feelings and thoughts about being teased or harassed. Perpetrators are characterised as 'pests' or 'bullies'. 'Bullies' victimise others by saying or doing unpleasant things and usually do not stop unless adults intervene. 'Pests' generally go along with a bully or are just silly and annoying and usually stop when asked. When children learn this difference, they can decide whether to stand up for themselves or get help from an adult. Hint Cards include humorous sayings that might be used to lighten up the situation. Children practise standing up for themselves without making things worse. The difference between being funny and being mean or sarcastic is explored.

Important: playing 'Tease' does not replace the responsibility of the school for stopping teasing and bullying and for providing interventions for the perpetrators.

Playground
'Playground' is designed for children aged 7 to 12 to address a range of issues from the playground. The game covers issues like teasing, anger management and friendliness. The aim is to collect Awards from the playground (in the centre of the board) while keeping out of trouble. Players experience the consequences of unfriendly behaviour and collect Calm Cards with strategies for avoiding trouble. 'Playground' is a great game to play at the end of a series – or maybe just for the fun of it.

Give Me Strength
'Give Me Strength' is a non-competitive game designed for groups of children between ages 8 and 14 but with potential for use with a wider range. The game focuses on friendly acts like giving compliments, waiting for others, discussing feelings, being kind and working together. Winning is not the object of the game. Positive qualities are recognised in others by giving Strength Cards to each other. Friendly and co-operative acts are built into the game for fun. 'Give Me Strength' is a great game to play at the end of a series of games or to help build group cohesion, or maybe just for the fun of it.

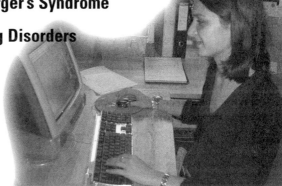